My Journey with Horses

CARMEN VOLZ

First published by Busybird Publishing 2025
Copyright © 2025 Carmen Volz

ISBN
Paperback: 978-1-923501-00-3
Ebook: 978-1-923501-01-0

This work is copyright. Apart from any use permitted under the Copyright Act 1968, no part of this publication may be reproduced, stored in a retrieval system or transmitted in any form or by any means, electronic, mechanical, photocopying, recording or otherwise, without the prior written permission of Carmen Volz. The information in this book is based on the author's experiences and opinions. The author and publisher disclaim responsibility for any adverse consequences, which may result from use of the information contained herein. Permission to use any external content has been sought by the author. Any breaches will be rectified in further editions of the book.

Cover design: Busybird Publishing

Layout and typesetting: Busybird Publishing

Busybird Publishing
2/118 Para Road
Montmorency, Victoria
Australia 3094
www.busybird.com.au

Content Warning

Readers are advised that the following memoir contains mature themes relating to death, grief, mental health, suicide and animal surgery including dissection.

For Panuk - I hope this helps make things better.

For my boys Liam, Ethan and Russell for supporting and loving me as I am.

Contents

Introduction	1
1 - Broken	7
2 - Where the passion began	17
3 - Our first horse Starbuck	23
4 - I don't fit in	35
5 - Teenage years	45
6 - I found my religion	57
7 - Matilda	77
8 - Education and clinic junkie	87
9 - I have a dream Giyabwe	97
10 - Breeding	103
11 - Life changes	109
12 - Railroad switch	119
13 - My new journey	129
14 - You are worth the world	135
15 - My new life	141
16 - Life as a trainer	153
17 - My big teachers	173
18 - Doing the miles	181
19 - The wheels began to wobble	195
20 - The fall begins	207
21 - Panuk	217
22 - The rabbit hole	225
23 - Rebuilding my happiness	239
24 - The world stood still	243
25 - What have I learnt?	249
26 - Where are things now?	255
References	259
Acknowledgements	260
About the Author	261

Introduction

Writing a book about my journey with horses has been on my bucket list for some time. Several lovely clients have asked me about my story and influences and the conversation almost always ends with, 'You should write a book.' In the hope of helping some people, or at least entertaining them, here we go. Not only am I fulfilling a dream, but I find telling a part of my story is incredible therapy for myself – and I hope for others, too.

There is nothing special about me technically, but we are all special in our own way. I don't compete. I am not famous or well-known. I do not have an amazing following on social media. I am not a big fan of social media at all. I am a normal (whatever that definition is) person who has had both highs and lows in my life. The one consistency has been being able to count on the balance and therapy of being with horses to get me through.

I committed myself to learning and educating myself, as much as possible, to obtain my dream job. That education helped me gain the confidence and expertise to create my own company doing what I love most – helping horses and people.

Horses have saved my life and made me the person I am. For that, I am forever indebted to them. Through my story, I hope others can see the benefit of believing in yourself. By educating your mind and listening to your heart, you can bring happiness and peace to a troubled soul.

I hope that reading my story will help you learn some horsemanship skills and understand that it is not just about how you are with horses but also about how you are in life.

I pride myself on delivering holistic care and have always tried to do what was right for both the horse and the person at the time. That holistic care is essential and I believe good training goes hand-in-hand with good horse management. I hope this approach will become apparent through some of the stories and horses' lives I have chosen to share.

To this day, I still feel I owe more to horses than what I have given them.

Trying to be a voice for horses is genuinely important to me. When things are not going right between the horse and the owner, I try to work out the problems and resolve them for both parties.

The issue can sometimes be a lack of communication, misunderstanding, pain or all three factors.

Throughout this book, I will mention some beautiful things I have witnessed and highlight those in the industry I respect. Unfortunately, like all industries, some do it more for the money and notoriety. I believe they can lose track of what is fair, respectful and realistic. Time, care, knowledge, experience and empathy go further than intimidation, control and lack of knowledge or skills.

At the end of the day, horses think differently than humans and I feel we owe it to them to try to think on their level to improve our understanding of them and treat them with greater respect.

Horses have an amazing nature and ability to be therapeutic in what can sometimes be a cruel world. During my years working with horses, I have incurred multiple injuries on my learning path. These include several concussions, internal bleeding, a broken nose, enduring the pain of having ligaments and tendons in my shoulders pulled to places they shouldn't be, experiencing displaced vertebrae in my neck, and the injury that led me to start my writing journey – tearing multiple ligaments in my knee and needing a complicated knee reconstruction.

But these injuries have taught me so much about risk management and how to work as safely as possible with horses. Appreciating that it is not a perfect science. At the end of the day, although you can take steps to minimise risks, there is sometimes just bad luck, and you are dealing with a prey animal.

I am not giving you a list of my injuries to wear as some sort of badge of honour, but more to explain the (sometimes *really* stupid) mistakes I have made and the lessons I have had to learn. Other times, I have been surprised that things have gone wrong but, truth be known, most of the time I could have seen it coming, I just needed to learn more. I have never met a better teacher than the horse.

The horse industry can be a rather hard place to work. For some reason, it tends to attract rather strong personalities. Everyone has their opinion, and some people can be overprotective, instead of open-minded, with their beliefs. As a good friend said to me once, 'Everyone has their own religion when it comes to horses.'

The industry has some amazing people – and I wouldn't have ever learned so much or been able to help others the way I do without their support, mentoring and knowledge.

Some of the vets and farriers out there are brilliant. Their care for horses is vital because the reality is that horses were not designed to be ridden or perform to the level of human expectations. As with all amazing athletes, giving them the best possible mental and physical opportunities to help them be able to do what we ask is the best gift we can give them. Horses will then have a better chance to enjoy their life and relationship with their human partner, while also minimising injury and enjoying a better chance at longevity.

I have probably spent well over one million dollars in my life so far on educating myself to spend my working and personal life with the creatures I love. Being a clinic junkie has been a significant part of that spending and it's seen me travel around Australia and America to learn what others do, attend seminars, enrol in university study, plus own, breed and start lots of horses. To start in the horse industry generally means training a horse to be ridden. It also includes first touching a horse, catching them and doing groundwork with them, generally leading them to accept and become comfortable with a rider. Who said education comes cheap? In saying this though, I strongly believe that it has been money well spent.

Do I wish I didn't have to pay hundreds of thousands of dollars in vet bills over the last 40 years? Definitely. Do I wish I hadn't seen trauma, cruelty, and probably watched well over 40-odd horses euthanised? Of course! Sadly, I still visualise and relive some of these in my mind today. But these experiences have also given me an incredible amount medically, biomechanically and spiritually, including a deeper understanding of the importance of trust in your training – and, boy, has it taught me to enjoy the moment and treasure those who are close to your heart.

I have gained such valuable, life-changing experience over the 40 years I have already shared with horses, but I also know I still have so much to learn. I often say to people when teaching, 'I am only telling you this because I have made the same mistake before and have learnt from it. I am just trying to make your path a little easier and more pleasant.'

I firmly believe all horses pick their owners to teach *them* something. It may not be what you wanted to learn, but what you *needed* to. Whenever I think of any horse I have had in my life, I can pretty much summarise instantly what they have taught me.

Growth, experience, and education are endless. Most great horsemen I respect grow older and hobble around with all their war wounds and unique personal learnings. They can be in their 80s and still saying, 'I am starting to understand some things now.' I always think, *man, do I still have so much to learn*, and if I stopped thinking that, I'd worry. When people come to one of my clinics, I always say that if everyone comes out uninjured, has learnt something and has a laugh, then I've done alright.

I hope this book can do this for you and thank you for taking a chance on me and giving my story your time and attention. I think time is one of the most precious gifts anyone can give, as time is never promised or limitless.

1

Broken

It was 10.45 am on Friday 28 May 2017 and I was waiting to go under a general anaesthetic for the second time in four weeks. Nerves and the fear of not knowing what the outcome would be rushed through me as I tried to be polite and confident with the staff, who were all so sympathetic and kind. The surgeon at St Vincent's Hospital in the leafy suburb of Kew assured me this time wouldn't be nearly as bad as the last time. However, he also said that, until he was able to feel my knee once I was under the general anaesthetic, he admitted he didn't know exactly what he would be doing. It could be anything from an MUA (manipulation under anaesthetic), cortisone and local injection, to an arthroscope with a 'clean out', or more.

All the questions went through my head again. Since my accident six weeks earlier, those same questions had run through my head constantly:

Why am I here?

What did I do wrong?

What did I miss?

Could this have been avoided?

Had I done the work I needed?

Maybe if our relationship was better?

Will I ever work again doing what I love?

Have I lost my credibility?

Am I being selfish to my boys?

Is this going to be used against me by one or two people who have been incredibly unkind to me?

Fear has a way of amplifying the voice of self-doubt ringing in my head. For that second time facing surgery, my thoughtful surgeon made sure I was booked in with the same team as the first time. They were all incredibly encouraging and kind, even deciding to waive their individual gap payments on the procedure, as they knew I had been through a rough trot (horse pun, can't help it) and was not able to be earning money.

Well, there I was, back on a trolley, getting wheeled into an operating theatre. At least the anaesthesiologist made better conversation that time, it almost seemed like we had started building a relationship.

As the IV line was placed into my skin, he smiled and said, 'See you on the other side.'

The liquid in the syringe was white. I'd never noticed that before. Oh, there was that cold feeling in my veins and …

I woke up in the recovery room, with a nurse telling me I was okay. Waking up from a general anaesthetic always leaves me crying and feeling scared. Of what exactly, I'm never sure. That time, I felt the pain and thought the surgeon must have had to go in again. My sobs punctuated the nurse's repeated question.

'What is your pain level from one to ten, ten being the worst?'

I'm never sure how to answer this question. I have two scales of pain level. There's the one when my first son was born after a difficult labour. I have never experienced anything like it since. When my second son arrived three years later, it was still painful but my body did its best to work through it and, in the scheme of things, it was considered 'textbook' and 'normal' by the supporting medical staff.

Then there are what I consider 'normal' pain levels. I pick the non-baby scale, otherwise I would never get past a two.

'Four to five,' I answered.

The nurse was quick to administer pain relief and constantly asked if I had any nausea. Obviously, they had been forewarned I was a chucker. No, no nausea, but still pain. The nurse rushed back and forth and called the anaesthesiologist for instructions. More pain relief was given.

I stared at the clock on the wall and worked out it'd been about 45 minutes since I woke. The pain had subsided. I still had no idea what had been done to my knee and I was still concerned. Then I saw my surgeon walk into the room with a big smile on his face.

'I thought you said you had to go?'

'Well, you were only under for a short time, and we got the best result,' he told me. 'So, I stayed to tell you myself.'

I liked that surgeon. I already had another appointment scheduled with him in two weeks, so he could have let the nurses tell me the results, but instead, he'd cared enough to stay.

That time, it was just an MUA, cortisone and a local in my knee. The surgeon proudly showed me some happy snaps of me under a general with him bending and straightening my leg. He explained that I had needed it and that it took a fair bit of persuasion to manipulate, including tearing through the scar tissue to get more movement. No wonder I was sore. He happily showed me my leg bent like a normal leg, and not quite straight. I reassured myself that I was clearly no wuss, even though it would still be a long road. I also decided I was thankful that I'd bought a new pair of white undies to wear to the hospital after seeing all those photos of me with my legs bent up in the air.

Two weeks later, I returned to the surgeon. It had been eight weeks since my accident when I was spun off a green horse. I think it was the initial staying on that caused my knee injury. Although all very fast, my mare spun once and I remembered leaning to the left and thinking, 'I am still on, I need to push down in my stirrup and get my balance back'. Then she spun again, and I was flung off.

I tore my anterior cruciate ligament (ACL) off the bone and down my femur, my medial collateral ligament (MLC) off the bone and my lateral collateral ligament (LCL) was slightly damaged, with some added bone bruising. The only way I could gain stability in my knee or walk again was to have a full knee reconstruction.

Never knew what a reconstruction was back then. Now I do. They cut pieces from your hamstrings and use them to create new attachments for your knee, then screw and staple them into place to replace the damaged ligaments. Sounds like fun, not.

I can honestly say that, next to having kids, it was the hardest physical thing I have gone through. In the first two weeks, you are only allowed to hobble to the bathroom using crutches and do your prescribed exercises. The rest of the time, you have your leg up, while in a full-leg brace that stays on for eight weeks after surgery. I have never taken so many pain killers in my life – and, boy, do they have some interesting side effects. I cried every day for the first six weeks.

But six weeks post-reconstruction surgery, and two weeks post-MUA, the surgeon, like the physio, was not happy again. I still had severe pain and couldn't bend much past 90 degrees in my left knee. I wondered if I'd ever be able to straighten my leg again. I was doing all the appropriate rehabilitation I was supposed to, but for some reason, my body had healed too quickly and grabbed onto everything and tightened, which can happen. The combination of crutches and the full-leg brace also restricted my movement as much as possible, to make sure all the machinery in my leg held my ligaments where they were meant to be.

I now have much more respect for footy players, who seem to move from knee reco's back to the footy field with relative ease. My surgeon had told me my injury was different from doing an ACL, but, even today, I still wince every time I watch footy and see someone bend the wrong way. Apparently, my knee looked like a car crash victim, and one of the worst he had seen. Thanks for sharing that little insight, Dr.

It was nine weeks since surgery, and the physio was playing with my leg and trying to bend it, while I tried to crawl off the bench to avoid the pain. Then the physio looked at me and said, 'I don't get it.'

'You are no wuss and you should be able to bend and straighten more.'

The physio asked me to pinpoint exactly where my knee hurt or felt tight. She then grabbed my kneecap and sort of lifted and tilted it.

She told me to try bending it again and, what do you know? I managed 15 degrees more bend immediately.

'OMG, how could I have missed it?!'

She grabbed the tape that footy players always seem to be covered in, then grabbed my kneecap and tilted and lifted it some more.

'Now try to bend.'

Yep, I managed a bit more. I had a subluxed kneecap, which may have happened at the time of the accident but can also happen after that type of surgery. (But don't quote me on this stuff.)

Since my quadriceps muscle had lost all its tone, it was more likely to be from after surgery. If you can imagine a pulley system with things out of alignment, that was me.

Yeah! (One of my favourite sayings!) I often use this saying when teaching a client who has had difficulty understanding something. When they finally get it I will scream in joy: 'Yeah!'

At least the physio worked it out. I just had to tape myself up every couple of days for a few months to help build the supportive structures that would help keep my kneecap where it was meant to be.

There is a reason I have babbled on about my knee but I will try to shut up about it going forward. It was a catalyst for change in my feelings of self-doubt. The change I didn't know at that stage. The whole time throughout the process of rehabilitation, I was thinking, 'poor horses' (yes, as all previous staff and my kids tell me, I relate everything to horses).

But poor horse owners, too. As working with people and horses is my job, I can't help but think this way. I had worked a lot with rehabilitating horses and trying to fix physical issues with horses, as it was affecting their behaviour and biomechanics. I knew how frustrating and difficult it was for trainers, vets and owners combined to (sometimes) work out problems. But man, I could talk. I was always talking to experts, telling them and even pointing to what hurt, but it still took them time to work things out. I was the man in the middle with horses and their owners; with rehabilitation journeys and knew the frustration. But with my knee injury, I had started truly living it myself.

Like all rehabilitation cases, the secondaries crept in thick and fast from trying to protect my left leg and getting the rest of my body to take more of the load. My hip started aching from swinging my deadweight leg. My lower back was too – everything that was over-compensating for my knee not doing its job was hurting.

Like most people who work outside and with horses, my body had been bashed about a bit. Before the accident, I had a sore shoulder and my right foot hurt putting shoes on, as well as every time I rose in my stirrups when riding. Like most people with their own business, though, I ignored all these aches and pains to avoid taking time off.

But putting a heavier load on my right leg and foot was making my right foot start to hurt as much as my left knee. Walking was becoming a sort of double limp. If you can imagine a constipated chook, that is sort of what I looked like. I couldn't bend my left knee properly and it hurt to land on my right foot.

Poor, poor horses, that have to put up with these aches and pains too often. At least I could speak. I've seen so many cases where a horse was lame in one leg and then another limb or hoof became a bigger issue.

It's given me an appreciation of how difficult it is for farriers and vets when a horse's gait doesn't look right, but they were not lame in just one limb. I had attended a biomechanic seminar in Atlanta, Georgia the previous year on this exact issue and had continued to take this most recent research back to the horses and people I worked with in Australia.

Now that knowledge was helping me manage my own injury, I knew that to prevent further damage to myself, I needed to focus on moving slowly and softly with good cadence. Talk about really getting into what you believe in – I was now living it with every step I tried to take.

So, off I went to the hospital again for x-rays on my foot. The radiologist advised me I needed to go to the emergency department, as the results were not normal. After sitting there for a bit, I got seen by a doctor who asked me if I drove in, as I may have to be plastered from toe to knee. The no-nonsense assessment gave me a mild panic attack, and I told them that

I wasn't really keen on this news, because there was no one to drive my kids around.

But they didn't seem too concerned about how I might manage the logistics of my daily life, and told me that I may have to be in a wheelchair for three months, as my left leg will not be strong enough yet to fully bear weight.

After years of ignoring all those aches and pains, they were coming back to haunt me – with a vengeance. The technical talk assessment of my issue was 'avulsed bony fragment of an adjacent cuboid with irregularity of the donor site'. I think that means 'piece of bone has broken off and left a rough bit where it came from'.

But there was more (WTF!). The doctor advised me he felt they were only seeing part of the puzzle and I needed to get an MRI and go back to the orthopaedic surgeon to get a complete and clearer picture of my injuries.

It made me think, *what would have happened if I was a horse?* (Yes, I am *always* thinking this way). My initial injury would have been picked up, as it was an obvious trauma and my knee did not look normal, but what about the secondary foot issue? Would I have been put down? If I had the surgery and recovery, I suspect I would have shut down mentally and gone quiet, as the thought of jogging or running was terrifying.

When I first got up in the morning I could barely walk. Then, once I warmed up, I was okay, even though I was in pain. As a horse, I would have possibly been known as a nice, reliable old thing. I guarantee you, though, if someone had jumped on my back, I would have gone as slow as possible and, only if the kicking or whipping of me was more painful than my injuries would I have moved any faster. I wouldn't even have had the grunt to buck, that would have just caused more pain for me.

Good thing for me I am not a horse, and had an amazing support network of caring, loving family and friends who saw me through that time.

As much as I questioned all sorts of things about why I was in this situation, the reality was that I just was. My body had gone through wear and tear over the years and the accident was just that: an accident. Maybe it could have been a different outcome if I had done all sorts of things differently.

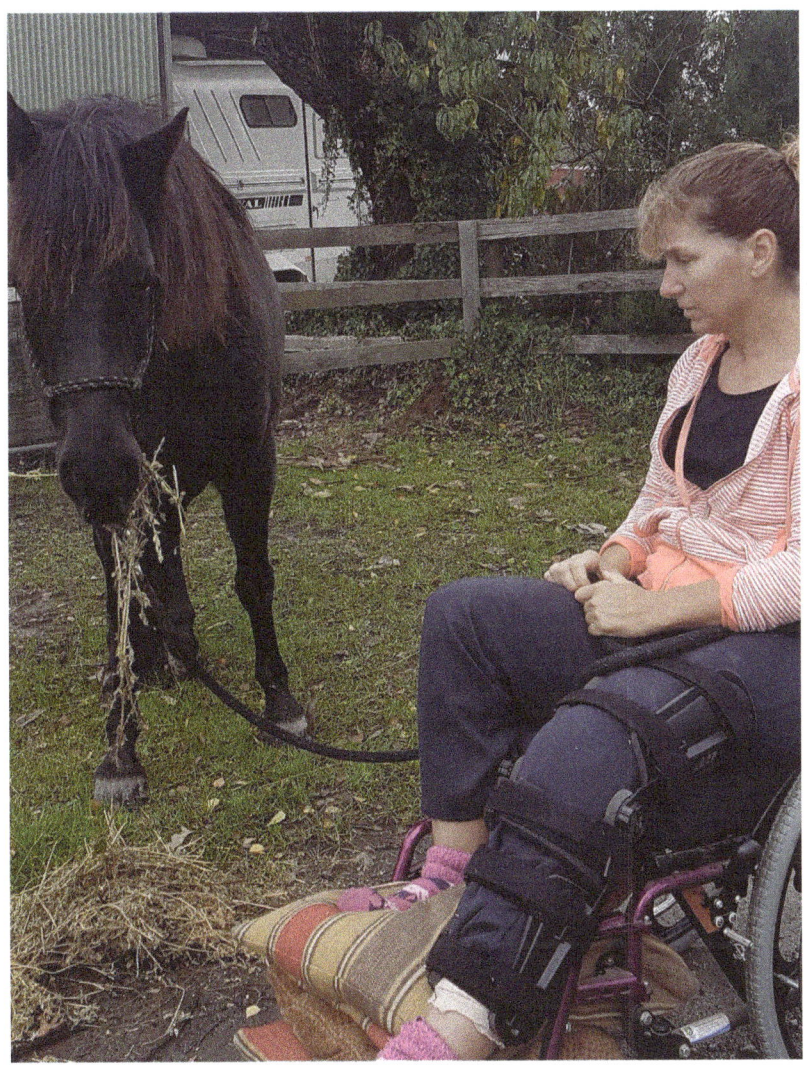

Recovery from accident with Bella

I had been questioning vets for years about the mare that I was riding when I had my accident. Probably bordering on stalking and telling them the behavioural signs I had experienced – whether they wanted to listen or not. But I couldn't change what had happened, just hopefully learn more from it. It is a dangerous job and I do my best to limit the risks and to keep learning constantly, but things can also just happen ... or so I thought.

So, it was off to the orthopaedic surgeon again in two weeks. The biggest blessing from the situation at that time was that it gave me the time and drive to write this book. So, let's go to where it all began ...

2

Where the passion began

I didn't have lots of friends at school, but the ones I did have were fantastic.

I put my lack of overwhelming popularity down to my tendency to be quite reserved. I was also a bit of a tomboy and didn't tolerate a lot of crap, as I had enough of that at home. Maybe that came across as a kind of toughness, or gruffness – I'm not sure.

Christine and I met when we were both eight years old and at the same school.

I'd never really noticed her before, but once I did, it was because she was different from the others. So unflinchingly honest. We shared a habit of not caring about fleeting trends, but just wanted to be active, have fun and be real. So, very quickly a great friendship began.

I can't remember when we started having sleepovers; we were almost inseparable. What I do remember is we stayed at Christine's house more than mine. Her house was a home – a safe and loving environment. Mine was not. Ever since my dad moved out of the house we lived in, I never felt safe. Dad used to give me crap about having nightmares and being scared through the night. In saying that, I used to sleep under the pool table in the rumpus room where he slept on the couch when he lived with us. That way I knew he was there to protect me. I noticed in Christine's household that things felt safe; there was this calmness. Her parents were so kind and so happy together. I always had a nervousness about me at my house, where I was prepared to run if I had to. I always had some type of anxiety everywhere, as I didn't trust many people.

I remember Christine ringing me one weekend when she said she was too busy to catch up because she was going on a horse ride and would call me later to tell me all about it. I remember the call back and the excitement in her voice: 'It was amazing – I know you will love it.' So, for her ninth birthday, her father, Fred, drove us both to a horse-riding school out at Lysterfield. I remember walking through all the horses while they were tied up and they all just seemed to be in a trance. Some were so big, some were ponies. But they were all so quiet. They had such big eyes, but they seemed to almost be distant. I was intrigued. I knew nothing about horses, and I was a little scared to ride one. I was put on Ajax. He was very old and skinny, and his bay coat was dull. They had a lead connected to his bridle and I thought this was ok, not too bouncy. They then undid the lead and let me steer Ajax myself, as well as stop and go. WOW!!!!! Now *this* was amazing.

Being on Ajax felt like an extension of my arms and legs but with another mind and soul attached. I couldn't believe these amazing animals were so compliant with our human demands. With me blundering around, this amazing creature still tried to understand my directions and help me learn how to communicate with him for the benefit of us both.

Horses don't lie. They want clear, honest, simple communication. They don't care what you look like, whether you're fat or thin, trendy, have lots of friends or the latest jeans. They don't yell at you, desert you or ignore you because they are so busy messing up their own life by being selfish. They don't go out partying and let their ego take control. Horses are honest, faithful, grateful, hardworking and, if you are fair, consistent and look after them, they will do almost anything to work with you – as long as there is nothing to fear. These animals have a greater sense of life, purpose and ethics than some people I knew who were adults when I was a child.

That was it. I could no longer survive my horrid world without these amazing animals. This gave me a window of hope outside of my home life. I felt I had no one to talk to at home, I felt alone. My mother was caught up in her own issues and there was no space for her to reassure me of life. Little did I know the bond and connection this initial adventure with horses would set me up for throughout my life. I had found my screening board, my grounding, my psychologist and an understanding of what was fair and what was not. Horses helped me set my guidelines for how I would try to live my life. Try, work hard and be kind and giving unless you are treated badly.

From that day, Christine and I were hooked. She told her parents that we wanted to do it weekly and also managed to convince them of the health benefits to help get our shared wish across the line. With some encouragement from Christine's mum and dad, Joan and Fred, my mum was soon on board too. Despite her flaws, Mum did have some very amiable qualities. She was very intelligent. She worked hard at her job as a psychiatric nurse and was intuitive about where people were emotionally. She was a strong supporter of all further education. I feel that, although she was incapable of emotionally or physically more with me at that time, she knew I needed something.

That is probably the thing I am most grateful for. Mum allowing me to pursue horses opened up a whole new world. From then on, we would go back to the riding school and go for an hour-long trail ride every Sunday. I would hover between riding Ben, Ajax, and Ringo. Ajax and Ringo were very similar.

Aged bay geldings that had been there done that and – now that I know more – were so tired, sore and shut down that they had learned life was easier for them when they just complied, regardless of how they were treated. Ben was different - he was my favourite. He wasn't that big but had an attitude and a presence. Ben was a brilliant, rather largish pony, who was quite push-button. If you knew what you were doing and could give him the right instructions, he was quite a great little horse. He taught me lots. From trying to race off to always wanting to be up front, to sweeping me off under a tree branch. Yep, I will never forget Ben and his funny sense of humour and how he taught me pretty quickly that, unless you communicate well and show your four-legged partner you need to lead, some horses can get rather tired of dealing with hopeless humans every weekend.

My sister Ruth began joining us on our weekly trek to the riding school. I think she initially just got sick of hearing me rabbit on about it and thought she'd better try it for herself. *Apparently, I rabbit on a lot about horse stuff* ... Once Ruth started, I'm pretty sure she felt the same as me. We never really discussed much about the specifics of what happened at home, as we both lived it. But we did talk about how unsafe our home environment was – and how anxious that made us. Horses were another world – a reliable but exciting one, with strong, loyal souls that could temporarily carry us away from our frustrating existence.

Sunday mornings very quickly became the time of the week we lived for. The riding school wouldn't allow any rides when the weather was too bad or wet and I remember sitting in my bedroom crying every time our Sunday ride was cancelled. I relied on that event – it was my sanity and, quite simply, the only place I felt safe. All my anxiety would disappear when I was with horses. It was like my heart rate dropped and I felt at peace. It was like a drug that left me feeling unjudged and euphoric. I felt I mattered and was part of my special, own world that others could only understand if they got the same rush. I wondered whether deep down, this is why Mum agreed to support this passion. It was a much healthier option than a chemical substance when someone was struggling.

3

Our first horse Starbuck

By the time I turned 11, I'd been going to the riding school religiously, every weekend, for three years.

Things at home were still very unstable and damaging. Horses, along with the other animals we had as pets, had very much become my only happy place. Mum must have been able to see this and decided to chat to the riding school about looking out for an appropriate first horse to buy for my sister and me to share. After several weeks, the riding school owner contacted my mother and told her they had swapped a horse with someone but were not able to use it as he 'was lazy'. Today, when someone uses this term for a horse, I know how ignorant they are. I have never met a lazy horse yet. A 'shut down' one? I have met plenty. A horse in pain? Too many. But never a lazy one.

The riding school also said, 'He did not like trail riding, and was not suitable for them.' This horse had been locked up in a concrete yard by the previous owners before the riding school and was in poor condition. My sister and I did not care, any horse was going to be the best horse for us. We waited until the following Sunday to see this horse and work out if we were going to get him.

His name was Starbuck. He was a three-year-old, 14.1hh buckskin gelding. Starbuck was so skinny I could poke my fingers in between his ribs. He had chunks of hair missing from his rump from lice and his eyes were dull. There was no usual behaviour of such a young horse as he simply had no will or energy.

The riding school were the horse's new owners now and they offered him to Mum for $250, as they thought he may not live too long. Still to this day, I don't know why the riding school owners convinced us to ride him that day. I cannot even remember who rode him first - my sister or me. I just remember thinking, *should we be doing this?* He seemed so depressed and soul-less. I remember being on him and he would only just walk. All the other horses were way out in front and I remember them going off without me and then picking us up on the way back, as we were that slow. I now know this story way too well. This was *not* lazy. This is what a 'shut down' horse is like when they are in so much pain that they just cop everything, without complaint. So, like most people with their first horse who know nothing, Mum bought him for us. The date was 3 November 1980 – and it was one of the happiest days of my life. Hope stretched out ahead of me. For the first time in such a long time, I had purpose.

We found an agistment property to keep him, then hired a float and hauled him back to his new home. We bought him a second-hand saddle, bridle, some new brushes – and me a book on caring for your horse. Starbuck learnt early that he was on a good wicket, even though, without knowing it, we were lucky to have not killed him.

I read that book from start to finish and then implemented everything I felt I had learnt. Every day, we went up to the agistment and would catch Starbuck. We would then lead him to the water trough, armed with a sponge, and wash his eyes, and nose and then dock, just like the book said (funny, hey?). We would then feed him two rather large buckets of Completo (a brand of pre-mixed horse feed), and, once he had finally eaten that, we would then saddle him up and ride him. Please remember I was only 11 years old and knew no better.

This continued for some months, and Starbuck was finally starting to get rounder and develop some attitude and energy (now that he wasn't about to drop dead). After months of treating the poor thing this way, Ruth and I were finally approached by one of the women at the agistment who had been staring at us with interest for some time.

I will never forget that conversation. It started with, 'Have you ever heard of a thing called Colic?'

We told her we hadn't.

Then, this lovely lady – I think, from memory, her name was Carol – just smiled at us, and explained a few basics of a horse's digestive system and that feeding after working Starbuck was better for him.

I was back on a mission and started reading everything I could find on horses and feeding, anatomy and how their bodies worked. It wasn't like how it is now with the internet and you just 'Google' things. I had to go to the library, borrow books from people and put in the legwork to find information. From then on, most birthdays and Christmases involved getting a new horse book if I was lucky – and that suited me perfectly.

Starbuck was pretty much a green horse and had two green owners. He wouldn't go when asked, only turned one way in preference, and would take off at the bottom of a hill. In reflection, he was a saint. Ruth and I would take turns to ride him and try to work these things out. All the common mistakes you could make with a horse, we pretty much made them. But it was when we started experimenting a little with our groundwork and riding that we noticed how things started changing. I was probably a little selfish with Starbuck and took over a little. Ruth felt he was better suited with me and, understandably, found him frustrating at times – so, she handed him over to me while she put the word out that she was looking for a cheap horse to buy.

I joined the local pony club and started riding out a lot. My whole weekend was spent at the horse paddock. Instead of relying on our older brother to drive us there, we started riding our push bikes to the paddock and back every day. Mum lost her licence, so could no longer drive us anywhere. Best thing that could have happened for everyone's safety on the road or in the car with her, but that is a different story.

Riding our push bikes every day from Mount Waverley to East Burwood became our daily routine. It seemed like a long way back then but googling now I see it was only 4.6 kilometres one way. I suppose when you look at it though, that was nine kilometres a day pushbike-riding, and endless hours horse-riding, no wonder I was so thin back then. Carrying feed buckets, as well as brushes and the bridle was a lot, so I started leaving the saddle behind as it was too difficult to lug around. Then, I decided the bridle was too annoying, so most of the time I rode bareback everywhere with just a halter and lead rope. I didn't know I was doing 'natural' horsemanship or anything special, I was just riding my horse. I think most kids start this way and it is only once we become adults that we start over-analysing things and understanding consequences.

We'd ride down the middle of Burwood Highway, which had six lanes and a median strip down the middle, then pull the horses up at major intersections to push the buttons on the traffic lights. We'd ride down to Jells Park, which had a great swimming hole. Ride to the shops to get fish and chips in winter and keep the paper package inside our coats to keep us warm. I found Starbuck the one male in my life, besides my father, my brothers, Christine's dad, Fred, and my dog, that I could trust. Looking at this from the outside, you might think I had a lot of male role models I could trust. I did. But, looking back, my perception was altered.

When I was four years old, there had been several incidents with an adult male neighbour. Inappropriate things. It is incredibly difficult as a four-year-old to work out when someone is kind, or when what they are doing is wrong. I do remember the look on his face, though. I worked out several years later what that look meant for a male and their intent. It has governed a lot of interactions with men that weren't family for the rest of my life.

With Starbuck, we taught each other the benefits of good communication – and the ultimate in trust. We both needed that.

Starbuck and I were never apart on weekends. Sometimes we'd ride out with others, sometimes by ourselves. There was open park and bushland with some riding tracks through it that we started going to, called Police Paddocks. Being the sort of neighbourhood it was, it also attracted other past times. We got used to avoiding the parked cars and motorbike riders who were not always horse-savvy.

There were also a couple of times with girlfriends when we'd been hassled by young blokes. Once, we had two young guys jump out of a car and threaten us. There were three of us there at the time, and although the blokes might have only been trying to get a reaction from us, threatening to pull teenage girls off their horses and rape them wasn't funny. The other girls brushed it off and we rode away without further incident, but it scared me.

I had started riding more and more by myself and I knew I wanted to keep riding there, so I decided it was time to give Starbuck a kind of self-defence mechanism for me because the truth was that I didn't trust most blokes.

I taught my wonderful horse to double-barrel (pig root) with both back feet and, like all bad habits you can teach horses, such as striking or rearing, it didn't take long for him to learn. I'd only been riding now for about five years and I worked out how to train him to do this within about five minutes. To me, it was simple. When I was on his back, I put both my feet back a little on him and squeezed just enough to annoy him and make him react. I continued with this, each time giving when I got a bigger response until his pig root was hard and high. I would never recommend teaching that sort of thing to a horse now – *professional ethics coming in now because I need to sound responsible* … but for me, at the time it was a matter of survival, yet again. These days, I get frustrated when I see horses rear on command or strike. It is such an easy thing to teach them and not always a desired trait but more a show bag (looks good but is full of shit) type of trick. But for me and Starbuck, it paid off. One day in late summer, I was riding in Police Paddocks by myself. It must have been just after lunchtime. It was a warm day, and I would normally only wear a singlet and shorts, but that day I'd dressed in jeans and had taken my saddle and bridle.

Starbuck and I had been enjoying a lovely ride when two guys on motorbikes showed up. Initially, they just rode past me slowly and because I was thankful for that, I waved a 'thank you' to them. Then I noticed them stop a bit further up the track, have a brief chat with each other, then turn around and come back toward me.

We were right in the centre part of the Police Paddocks. At first, they just circled me – I guessed to see if my horse was reactive to their motorbikes or not. Luckily for me, I had previously ridden in a group where one of the guys was on a motorbike while a couple of us were on horses, so Starbuck was used to the noise of the engines and not too fussed. But because he was now picking up on my nervousness, he changed from quiet to a little pumped and waiting for my cue on what to do. The guys stopped their motorbikes. They then began the normal pick-up line crap with me. To this day I still get annoyed by creeps.

'Have you got the time?' one asked. I replied nervously.

'Do you want to get off your horse and come sit with us?' Alarm Bell City.

I can't remember my exact response, but it was something like, 'No, I just need to keep riding.'

One of them became immediately aggressive, telling me they would just follow me until I gave in.

'Who knows what we might do? What do you think we will do to you?'

By now, I was freaking out and having visions of being dragged off Starbuck and being raped and bashed. I was nervous but I knew I had to give myself one more try to get out of the situation.

'I need to go,' I told them, as I started riding away, closer to the less aggressive of the two guys. Just as I was about to ride past, he went to grab the reins and Starbuck shied a little, as he was also wary of most blokes. It was only a little shy, but just enough for the guy to pull back – thankfully, he seemed a little nervy of horses. So, I half-turned Starbuck and put my feet back. As we had practised so many times, he double-barrelled on command. With that, the guy started running backwards, I backed Starbuck up and put my feet back again.

Crack! Smash! Starbuck was shod, so the noise of his hooves hitting the motorbike was loud – and the force was enough to push the bike over.

When it hit the ground, I saw some sort of liquid spreading across the dirt, but I wasn't sure what it was or if anything serious was broken. The guys started swearing at me and running at the bike, so I took off. We galloped as fast as we

Teaching Starbuck to pigroot

could, while still checking Starbuck back to manage the bends in the track. I then slowed to a fast canter, realising I wasn't that good a rider and that it was more important to manage the track and stay on, rather than panic Starbuck.

We were quite a distance away when I heard one motorbike starting up, and then coming in our direction. I didn't know if one or two motorbikes were coming and I didn't care. I was so scared. The bush had thickened a little on the side of the track, so I slowed down and snuck off away from the track and hid. By the way, hiding a horse is no small feat. But there was a small patch of flattened grass behind a clump of trees and bushes just off the track. There was only one motorbike, and it went back and forth slowly a couple of times. Lucky for us, the guy on the bike could not hear our breathing over the sound of his motorbike's engine. I waited more than 30 minutes before I thought it was safe enough and crept out.

I'd never been so scared in my life and the fear stayed with me as I rode back through the quiet parts of the track, towards home – convinced they were going to find me.

But once back on the bitumen roads, I knew we had made it, as there were so many cars around, I was confident I could have flagged someone down to help.

Once we were back in the paddock, I untacked Starbuck, washed him down, gave him his feed. I then put his halter on and walked him to a big patch of grass just outside the paddock to let him graze on the beautiful green grass on the edges of the sports oval. I pulled my jeans up and saw the rash on my legs from riding so hard for so long and the skin that was rubbed raw from my jeans. Shorts would have been way worse. I then broke down and just cried, hiding my face in Starbuck's mane. This was my safe place. The smell of a horse always seemed safe – like my own private world where no one could hurt me. This amazing horse had just saved me. He knew I was nervous and scared of the guys and had worked with me by doing everything I asked of him. Because of that, we were safe. I loved this horse more than I thought was possible. I didn't want to go home, as there was no one besides my sister and Christine I could talk to about it. But not only that, I didn't want to leave Starbuck. He knew what we had just been through, and he was there for me.

***

Time went by and Starbuck and I started doing more. As part of the pony club, we started competing a little, going to games days, and one-day eventing.

My sister, Ruth, had found another horse, Banjo. He'd also been neglected and was agisted in the same place as Starbuck. Ruth asked his owner if she could start feeding and working him and the owner was happy with this because she didn't have time for him. Within a week or so, Banjo disappeared from the paddock. Ruth rang the owner to ask what had happened and found out someone called the RSPCA and she had surrendered Banjo to them. Banjo's owner told Ruth that if she wanted him, she could have him. All my sister had to do was give the woman $20 and pay his vet bill from the RSPCA.

A few days later, we went down there and, once the RSPCA was happy with us and Banjo's condition had improved, they released him to us. The vet bill was $72. To this day, I think that is one of the best purchases ever made. Again, our mum was happy to pay for this and to finance us now having two horses. It's a decision I'm forever grateful for. Ruth never paid that $20 to the owner but the 15.1hh, five-year-old brown gelding was hers. Although incredibly skinny, lice and worm-ridden, he had a presence and looked either Anglo/Arab-cross or Andalusian-cross. He was magnificent. It took Ruth some months to rehabilitate him, but he soon looked amazing. We became better at rehabbing horses. Banjo was a whole different ball game to work with and ride than Starbuck ever was. And so, *their* journey began.

I hadn't been back riding down Police Paddocks and had warned all the other girls at the agistment about what had happened to me. I never went to the police and never even thought of reporting what had happened, as I hadn't even told my parents. Quite simply, I was young and dumb and thought that no one at home would care. I often thought that, when stuff like that happened, it was just something you had to deal with. The world was not always a nice place. I then heard on the radio that there had been a couple of reports of rape at the police paddocks. Girls had been picked up from somewhere else and then taken there. There had also been reports of fishing line being tied up high between trees, so that if horse-riders were going through, they would strike it, and, at worse, perhaps be decapitated.

I felt sick and cried. I could never understand why some people were so twisted. A wave of guilt also ran across me. If I had only been brave enough to tell others. That whole event had a massive impact on me. I felt this immense responsibility that, in future, I needed to speak up.

4

I don't fit in

I was keen to advance Starbuck and would attend the local pony club with a couple of the girls whose horses shared the same agistment property with Starbuck. It was handy because it was only a 30-minute horse ride from the paddock.

But it was a different world. A couple of the instructors were lovely and encouraging and knew way more than I thought I would *ever* know. I found some instructors very frustrating as they couldn't answer my questions – and when they tried to, nothing they said made any sense to me. Probably the most frustrating thing was that some didn't seem to care for the horses that surrounded them. For them, it was more about what you could do on a horse. Not what you could do for the horse.

I lost count of how many times I was told I had 'potential' but needed another horse to help me fulfil it. But I loved the horse I had. I did *not* want to 'upgrade'. I entered a few one-day events and placed third a few times. At the end of my dressage test, I would always get asked if my horse was lame on all four feet because of his weird canter, but to this day I still believe he wasn't. Starbuck was the soundest horse I think I have owned and was still a great riding horse into his 20s. I found a lot of the pony club rules frustrating because again, the questions I had about how a horse thinks, trains and communicates weren't being addressed.

Starbuck at agistment after Pony Club

Around this time, I met a 'cowboy' named Manny. He owned a magnificent horse called Shilo. Manny was short for Emmanuel. I think he was of Mexican descent. I can recall a bronzed man with a dark moustache and cream cowboy hat and a beautiful, tall bay gelding. I remember watching him ride and it was like watching two entwined souls that knew exactly what the other was thinking. Shilo got loose one day near the footy oval while Manny was letting him graze without holding the rope. He got a fright and startled a little and trotted away a bit. It's all a bit foggy in my memory now, but I remember telling Manny that Shilo was loose.

What happened next is something I will never forget – and if you ever read this, Manny, THANK YOU for showing me how and what a real relationship was like.

Manny simply made some sort of gesture and noise. Even from his distance, Shilo immediately took note and came calmly back, then dropped his head to Manny for a scratch. WTF? I wanted that. *Welcome to liberty training*.

A lot of the girls at the agistment started bugging Manny to help us work with our horses. He never directly worked with us, or so I thought, but said, 'If you want to come out riding with me, you need to be able to fall off.'

I thought he was asking us to be like crash test dummies until he explained.

He wanted to see us work with our horses to the point we could feel and anticipate when something was wrong, and act accordingly.

Starbuck and I now had a goal. I needed to be able to canter bareback, then dismount without getting hurt and without giving Starbuck a hard time or wrenching on his mouth.

A few of us girls worked together initially to try to reach our goal, but I became a little obsessed with achieving this. This simple little exercise that Manny had asked us to do set me off to explore all sorts of things. Later in life, I was blessed to watch a Ray Hunt clinic where he would often say, 'It's what happens before it happens, happens.' I reflected on my time training Starbuck when I heard this saying, and it was only then that the power of these few words concreted in my somewhat thick brain.

Starbuck and I started slow with our task. To start with, from a standstill, I would lean forward on Starbuck's neck and then wrap my arms around him, jump off and land on my feet. We progressed to do this from a walk, then a trot, and then a canter. The mutual understanding that Starbuck and I had developed was so good that we got this to the point where I would only get as far as leaning forward and starting to hook my arms before he would immediately stop and arc his neck towards me to make a safe little pocket for me to land. He would even support me to stay upright. I still miss him terribly – to this day.

This sort of stuff was getting into my blood. I am not saying that all the dressage, jumping, cross country and other stuff at pony club didn't need this level of understanding, there was just no one there I admired in the same way I looked up to Manny and his methods. It was then that I realised. If you see something you admire, go see how they do it. For me, it was my perceptions of those entwined souls. It was the first time I had watched someone with a horse and almost believed they were one. Bottom-half horse, top-half human. In between, their heart and soul were one. The mutual love, respect, trust and understanding just oozed from their eyes and watching them work together was so inspiring. That is what I wanted. What Manny and Shilo had.

***

I continued with pony club, even though it just didn't feel right. I never understood why I was getting told about needing another bit, noseband, or martingale. I didn't get it. I knew when

I had things right with Starbuck, I could ride him halter and bareback and achieve anything. I was starting to become a bit of a horse-riding rebel. I went to a few shows but found it very stuck up and not a supportive environment. Especially when I had shabby-looking buckskin and no flash gear or clothes. We didn't own a float and, even if I hired one, there was nobody to tow it.

The only show I went to besides our pony club was when I paid a friend's mum to take me with her daughter who was also going. That day, Starbuck was lame when I started doing a dressage test, so that finished that for the day. The girlfriend I went with let me ride her horse Bobby in the bareback event, which I thought was incredibly sharing and kind. I liked Susan. Later, I heard that either she or her mum thought the money I paid them to take me and stay the night at their place wasn't enough. I was devastated. I couldn't ask Mum for more money and I felt so guilty and embarrassed that it ended our friendship.

After that, the only shows I went to were ones I could ride myself to. I would go extra early to allow time to ride to the shows the pony club had and I'd carry a backpack with my brushes and other bits and pieces. Invariably, it meant that something was always forgotten, as I was trying to do too much all by myself.

To set the scene properly, we are talking about a forgetful, hormonal teenager. One day, I forgot my keys and because the agistment had a padlock on the gate to get out, we were stuck. But because Starbuck and I had worked so hard, I really wanted to get to the games day they had on.

Barbed wire fencing was not solid. We'd been doing some amazing jumping together and, with that in mind, I took my rug and placed it over the fence, then grabbed a pole and put it at the base and thought, *now it looks like a jump*. The top strand of barbed wire was a little loose in one area between two star-pickets that were ever so slightly lower. The other side was a raised dirt landing, so it was like jumping over and up an embankment. Quite a big ask, if I think about it now.

I had so much trust in Starbuck that it never occurred to me what I was asking. So, off we went to do a five-minute warm-up. Then, without any hesitation from either of us, I cantered straight at the fence. We cleared it easily. From then on, I never brought my key, I just always had a spare jumper I would throw over the fence. Starbuck never jumped the fence to leave the property without me there and always knew once the jumper went on the fence and I jumped on, it was time to do our stuff. *I know it was not a responsible thing to train but, gee, I was proud of us. Yes, probably good luck though he never got out with other agisters throwing rugs over the fence and then other horses flying up behind him at feed times.*

***

In those early teenage years, I remember the heavy impact others had on me without me realising it at the time. I was trying to get Starbuck fitter without always riding him, so I started to lunge him. I had no idea what I was doing and we fumbled around with him stopping, starting and showing no consistency at all.

This went on for a couple of sessions until I decided it wasn't working – and that I needed to try something else. One of the ladies at our agistment made comments to me along the lines of, 'That doesn't look any good, you are just confusing the poor horse.' Which was true, but because it was said down her nose at me, I didn't want to listen. She was a lot older and was always in jodhpurs and picture-perfect. Her horse was over 16hh – big, immaculately groomed and always in the perfect rug combination. I think I didn't like her more out of jealousy than anything. I started to get quite judgemental about horsewomen in the perfect outfit that looked like they had a pole jammed up their backside.

I worked with Starbuck and broke things down into bite-sized achievements – like that saying about how to eat an elephant one bite at a time. I also let go of my feelings of frustration and, whether my training session was five minutes long or an hour, we quit when things were good and we both understood. I still do both of those things today if things go off the rails a little. One bite or small achievement at a time, being sure to give time and just 'be' when there is a big change and realisation for the horse you are working with.

Within just over a week, Starbuck and I had lunging at a good level. We had clear, soft communication where I could signal him to walk, trot, or canter both ways and Starbuck would hold a slow steady pace and only change gait if asked.

The lady at the agistment who had previously commented to me stopped and watched. After a few minutes, she turned and said, 'Nice change.' It made my day. She even smiled, that pole dislodged. Now that I think about it, she didn't have a pole stuck up her backside, she probably just felt sorry for Starbuck and was frustrated by seeing what I was doing.

I continued my slightly rebellious ways but felt Starbuck and I had some great stuff going on. The last time I saw the older lady at the agistment with her big, expensive, colour-coordinated horse probably had a bigger impact on me.

It was one of those beautifully calm summer days where everyone was out riding their horses, but, because a thunderstorm was coming, most didn't leave the agistment. I was doing some flat work on Starbuck in a dirt arena where I had marked out the edges and letters with stones. Next to my pretend arena were several jumps made up of 44-gallon barrels on their side, plus some other jumps with tyres. The older lady was there riding her horse and doing a small jump course. The pole must have been implanted again because she was rudely explaining to me that Starbuck and I needed to leave, as we were in the way of her practice on her competition horse and that was more important. *Hello, red rag to a bull.*

    I questioned why her work with her horse was more important than mine. She answered that she competed and was at a higher level than me. She then proceeded to tell me my horse wasn't as good as hers and that hers was more expensive and better educated. I answered that her horse was bigger but mine would beat her hands down out of heart and soul. This then led to a jump-off. Remember Starbuck was 14.1hh and her horse was over 16hh. We started with jumps of barrels lying flat and we both easily cleared them. The lady then turned around and said, 'Well, I will jump a barrel standing upright,' thinking I wouldn't even challenge that. She set up the barrel, placed a pole on it, did her canter circle and the perfect line-up to the jump, and cleared it beautifully. She then went to ride off – no doubt thinking she had won. I was an angry, lonely teenager who just had someone tell me my relationship with my saviour was not as good as theirs. Not a chance I was letting that one go. I yelled out and said I would jump the same barrel upright with two tyres stacked on top. They were normal car tyres, not like truck tyres. It was a decent amount higher, though. I then jumped off and took my saddle and bridle off. All Starbuck had on was his halter and lead rope tied into reins. I rode like this a lot more than with a saddle and bridle and thought I was giving Starbuck the best chance with me balancing. Not only that, I had never seen this lady ride without a saddle and bridle.

    We set off in a relaxed canter and I followed the same circle and then the straight line of the lady. I was not nervous, scared or concerned at all. I had so much faith in our relationship and the training we had done to date.

When Starbuck pushed off his back feet, I remember thinking, *wow he is strong, we are going to clear this easy.*

We sailed through the air and made the perfect landing. I then walked up to the lady, who looked rather shell-shocked. 'You're an idiot,' she said, smiling. 'You may not be conventional, but you have your way. Your horse loves it.'

I will never forget her. She had a tear in her eye when she talked to me. I had no idea what was going on in her life, and obviously, she had stuff like everyone does. Her horse was her outlet too. I had threatened their bond. She felt judged by me. I had been too wrapped up in my own story to realise they had a story too.

'I have a lot going on in my life at the moment. Work, and man issues. You will encounter them in the future.' She laughed.

'I need an agistment with better facilities, and closer to work.'

She didn't always have a stick up her backside. Horses were her therapy too. She was a lovely lady and gave me some important advice.

'Stick to what you believe, you don't fit in with what I have experienced with horses. You are passionate about what to do and what you believe in. Be true to you.'

That was the last time I saw her. I didn't even know her name. Clever lady. I hope she has had a lovely life.

5

Teenage years

I continued to live for riding Starbuck. School wasn't that great. Teachers were always pushing me to know what was going on at home. They could tell from both my older sisters that none of us lacked intelligence, but other factors stopped us from excelling. I can never remember feeling relaxed or comfortable enough at home to do any homework. I would do anything to not be at home. If not going to the agistment to be with Starbuck, I would be at Christine's house or walking our dog. I was still best friends with Christine, and we went to the same high school together - a private catholic ladies' college, to be exact. Both Mum and Dad had their issues but both strongly believed that education and knowledge were key. Mum believed private schooling was the best option. I was lucky both Mum and Dad were both good workers in their careers and had the funds to support all of us five kids with the education they felt was the best.

***

We met two other lifelong friends there in year nine, Monique and Janine. Christine and Janine went to riding schools on the weekends and Monique and I had our horses at the same agistment. Out of the four of us, I was the least keen on boys and the most reserved. I was always a bit scared of being used or mistreated, but hormones do kick in ... *let's leave it at that, ladies... I think I'm safe unless one of the three of them also writes a book.* As for the other three girls, they were the best entertainment ever. We are all still friends now and their dancing skills and humour haven't changed. We still meet up to this day and fill each other in on our lives and families in between good food and wine. I could never imagine ever being without these friends in the future.

We have seen each other at our worst and celebrated with each other our special moments in life. We all know each other, warts and all, have celebrated births, marriages and deaths, and still instantly feel warmth and comfort when we see each other. Janine joked with me the other day that once this book is written, and a movie made, *realistically, just publishing this book will make me stoked enough,* she would like to be played by Toni Collette.

***

Dad had moved out of the house when I was eight and all five of us kids lived with Mum. Back then, kids in separated families rarely lived with their fathers. There was a discussion one day when our parents split, where our mum told us we would have to go to court and tell the judge which parent we would choose to live with. Boy, did that start a debate among us kids! I always felt, whether accurate or not, that our eldest brother and sister were Mum's favourites – both had been given Irish names. Mum was Irish. My other brother and sister were Dad's favourites – both had been given German names. Dad was German. My name was Spanish, apparently after distant relatives' nationality on Mum's side, even though my dad swore it was Ethiopian and not Spanish heritage. I don't know why he thought this, it was probably just to have fun with me.

It was a horrible time. I felt safer with Dad, but he was a strict man and was not happy. I had also been incredibly frightened by Dad, even though he always thought he was doing the best thing for us. One time in the past, the neighbours had told him that one of us had been setting off firecrackers, which we had been told not to do. He asked us who had done it and none of us would own up. I think it was my second brother, he was a bit of a rebel. *Must remember to ask him now.* Anyhow, as Dad didn't know who was responsible, he punished us all. He also said, 'From now on, if any of you do the wrong thing, all five of you will get consequences, as you need to stick together.' All five of us were lined up and got the strap. I felt that was incredibly mean, but in Dad's eyes, he had known he was going to leave and wanted us kids to be loyal and look after each other.

This is a man who grew up listening to Hitler on the radio in Germany. He was a very decent man and would do anything for his family but was in a torturous relationship with our mother. Other things occurred that I know would not be seen as the right thing, but his heart and head always thought it was. Dad gave a mortgage-free home to our mum and made her promise the door would always be open for us kids. He left with a Volkswagen beetle and two thousand dollars and started his life again at the age of 48.

Mum continued down her destructive path. Now that there was no one other than five young children to watch what she did, she didn't attempt to hide her party time. How she held onto full-time employment, I will never know. She would disappear for up to five days straight, leaving us all to look after ourselves.

One thing I remember most from our sporadic conversations was her telling us, 'There's money on the bench.'

We had a dirty ceramic bowl where loose change was thrown in. When Mum was going on a bender, she at least had the presence of mind (mostly!) to throw some notes in for us to live off.

And there my abandonment issues began. Time, care and being there are more important than money in my view.

Occasionally, we would receive the drunken phone call, but normally only got contact when she was back at work. She mainly worked night shift, so even when she was home, we would have to tiptoe around so she could sleep. If you woke her, it was very much like waking the sleeping dragon. Mum was a messy drunk. Beer would make her sleepy and sluggish. Spirits would fire her up and make her unpredictable, like an angry snake. I remember my sister once took the drawer beside Mum's bed to a pharmacist friend and asked them to go through what pills she was taking. Once they calculated everything, they asked how many people were taking these and said, 'Surely, they are not still alive.'

I know having five kids and being single would have been hard, but the wheels had started to wobble straight after I was born, if not well before. I wish someone could have helped her. I wish things didn't continue in such a destructive way. Dad had tried in several ways. Some personalities and people are just more prone to substance abuse, instead of dealing appropriately with their mental health. I am glad that mental health is now taken far more seriously and dealt with better, but there is still a long way to go and, quite simply, sometimes people can't find peace, no matter how much support they are offered. Despite her failings, we all stayed with Mum, as Dad told us to and, that way, we avoided the stress of court.

In my teenage years I was growing out of my tomboy ways, but feeling the whole lack of confidence that no boy would ever be interested in me anyway. I was 14 when I started seeing an older man.

Wrong fit for me but I was happy someone acted like they cared for me. My mother instantly disapproved and voiced her concerns. I was banned from going out and had to have my sister chaperone me to go to the agistment to see Starbuck. This was not great for our relationship, but my sister could also see I was slipping into the wrong crowd. Looking back, if one of my boys started seeing a 23-year-old woman when they were only 14, I would go nuts.

Like some teenagers do when they don't feel loved and supported at home, I ran away. I stayed at a friend's place whose parents were away and tried to work out what to do.

When I did call my home and one of my sisters answered, I told her that I was safe and that I would call in a few days. I wasn't old enough to get a job and I couldn't support having Starbuck. I rang Mum a few days later and tried to talk to her but she wasn't interested and just told me to get back home or she would make me a ward of the state.

I arranged a meeting with a government counsellor through a free legal aid service. This man showed me around a youth centre called 'Turana', where he explained I would more than likely end up if not fostered out at 14. It was scary. This was a sliding doors moment, where I could continue to rebel, or change. The youth worker put it simply: if I wasn't getting sexually or physically abused, put up with it. Lie if you must, get a part-time job and save to aim to leave home at 17 years old when the government wouldn't bother looking at me if Mum wanted to make me a ward of the state.

So, that's what I did.

I got a part-time job at McDonalds at the age of 15 and started to save. I stopped going to pony club and any sort of competing with horses, as I still felt I didn't fit in and there was discrimination. Horses are an expensive hobby. Ruth and I had the funds provided to us but never the time of a parent. Dad was always working and no longer living with us, so it was difficult to support us, timewise. Mum was always working or, if not, she was partying or self-medicating. Either with others or alone. I was the only kid at pony club who didn't have a parent there. A couple of times, Starbuck wasn't up for going to pony club, so my sister lent me her horse Banjo. Banjo now looked amazing and held himself incredibly well.

I remember all the attention I got from the instructors the times I took him instead of Starbuck and it annoyed me, as I had lots more going with Starbuck. It wasn't a 'hey, we can help you with the next level horse' thing. It was more like me thinking 'he looks better and is bigger, so let's show you off rather than help you'. Maybe it was just my thoughts creating this story in my head. I thought they missed a real opportunity to help me, as he was a very different horse to Starbuck, and I could have done a lot of things better.

After the last games day at our local pony club, where I cleaned up on everything Starbuck and I entered, I had one of the women on the committee come and chat with me. In short, I was getting offered a position on the club's games team if I could get all new equipment, including a new horse and a reliable parent or adult with a float to drive us to every competition. Like that was ever going to happen! It just put me off.

I didn't want everyone to know why my parents had never come to pony club or never seen me ride and why I didn't have some amazing relative who had a float and funds to support me. But the biggest issue was that I felt I wasn't learning anything, nor did anyone care that I wasn't, so I left. *And you wonder why I try to help teenagers now with open arms.*

I split up with that older man after I found out he was seeing one of my friends at the agistment at the same time as me. It hurt. Not the splitting up with him, but, yet again, I felt no one cared about me enough to stay with their whole heart. *If I could speak to myself now as a teenager I would say, 'He didn't deserve you, you rock and don't ever believe you are not good enough.'*

***

I continued to ride and train Starbuck and do anything and everything I could to learn more. Christine was dating a young man and wanted to set me up with his best friend. I was dead against this, and, truth be known, just wanted to play with my horse, work and get out of home. But, as best friends do, we got picked up one day from school by her boyfriend with his mate in the back seat of the car. I was shy and this was confronting for me to be in the back seat of a Gemini sedan in my short summer school uniform. I was incredibly embarrassed. I was 15 and this young man was 18 and at university. I was smitten and always wondered how someone so smart could be interested in me. I had no self-esteem – but he was interested. This is the man I married when I was 21 years old.

But despite our feelings for each other when we were young and still dating, both my parents were not fond of my choice. My mum banned me from seeing him.

I was told through various sources he was too smart and good-looking for me, and that while he was at university he would be getting better offers from older women, so I was best to let him go. *Go figure, I held on with both hands, with all my abandonment issues still there. PS: I was worth everything – what crap to tell someone!*

This man's mother was a wonderful woman and supported our relationship. I shared my plan with her that I was saving to move out at 17 and so she helped me. I had bought a couch, cutlery, crockery, and various other items and kept them at her house. I now decided to leave school, even though I had just started year twelve. I knew I had to work full-time to leave home, although secretly I wanted to go to university and become a vet.

During my brief time in year twelve, it was the first time I saw the teachers change in how they treated students. It was way more relaxed and friendly, with everyone knowing that, if you had made it this far in school, you were serious about getting through the final year.

I didn't want to leave school, as I genuinely loved learning, but with no safe support network, I couldn't see the point. I felt my mental health would suffer further if I stayed at home. I was two weeks into the school year when I explained to my mum I wasn't interested in school. *Yep, another lie.* She accepted this quite easily which surprised me. Mum valued a good education, and that's why she thought it was important for all of us kids to go to private schools.

School, on the other hand, did not accept it as easily. One teacher stood out. She had already given me a hard time before and, one day when I wagged school, she had rung my home and when I answered she said I didn't sound that sick and if I didn't come straight to school, she would have me expelled. That was in year ten. She was a teacher that cared, now that I look back, and was doing the whole tough love thing, but there was no way I was breaking my silence to reveal the truth about my home life. My four brothers and sisters before me kept their mouths closed and I felt it was also my duty to do the same.

The day I went in to advise the school I was leaving, I was three weeks into year twelve. I told the principal first, who again tried to get me to speak about the truth. I softened a little with her and just said that I knew nothing could be changed and I was getting the help I needed out of school.

When it came to going into the classroom for the very last time and getting my things, my homeroom teacher who had previously given me a hard time stopped the class. All her other tactics of getting me to tell the truth had not worked, so this time she tried to shame me. She asked me to tell everyone in the class why I was leaving. I simply said I was going to work in a retail shop and so didn't need to stay at school.

She announced to everyone, 'How is it that Carmen, being a very bright girl, is leaving school to work in a shop? Not a great career and something to aspire to, but you wreck your life and give up.'

I left the classroom embarrassed. I know she wanted me to feel shame for my choice, but my mental health and plan of getting out of home were more important. Might I also add, there is nothing wrong with working in a shop. If it makes you happy, good on you. But I would go nuts being nice to people all day.

I first worked in a gift shop in retail, where I had a lovely boss. The job wasn't exciting, but I stayed for about six months, as my boss was so kind. I then got a job working in a bakery. I contemplated being a pastry chef but stayed in front of the counter. I had just turned 17.

***

One night, I had my boyfriend over at home and we were in the bedroom I shared with my sister. He was sitting on the bed, and I was lying down, and we were talking. Fully clothed, with nothing going on. My mum burst through the door in a rage and just started yelling. She was not happy with me and accused me of all sorts of things and told me to leave home. The next day I did. One of the ladies I worked with at the bakery kindly let me move in with her and sleep on the couch, as I hadn't fully saved up the bond, as well as the first month's rent needed for a rental.

I lived with my work friend for three months. I didn't enjoy living there, because back in the 1980s, it was a rough suburb. In the time I lived in Bayswater, I was flashed at twice, plus I was followed and had a knife pulled on me – all on my way home. I was very scared and just wanted my own place.

After three months, I now had enough money for a rental in Murrumbeena, closer to the city and in what I believed was a safer suburb. Being only 17, they wouldn't let me sign a bond and agreement by myself so I contacted my dad and asked if he would do it on my behalf.

I will never forget the day he came around and saw where I was living in Bayswater. He had been misinformed about why I had been kicked out of home and initially was not willing to help.

My dad always respected the truth and, as we became adults, it became more obvious how much of a fair man he was. He was also a lot happier not living with Mum. I told Dad the full truth about a lot of things. He was so kind and supportive. That day changed our relationship.

I would always ring Dad and tell him exactly what was happening in my life from then on, and he would be honest back, some of which I didn't always want to hear, but his intentions were always good. Dad became a guarantor on a flat for me so I could move into my own place.

Home became a one-bedroom flat in Murrumbeena. I relied on my boyfriend and my sister to drive me back and forth to the agistment where Starbuck and Banjo were. My boyfriend wanted to move in, but he was still in university earning no money. I was working full-time, plus had two part-time jobs and couldn't afford anything more.

I didn't go out much and party, as I couldn't afford to and barely had any time off work. The only spare time I had, I would spend riding. I did love camping though and had a goal that I would eventually own a float and car capable of towing it and take Starbuck away with us on holidays.

When I turned 18, my boyfriend moved in and, with a double income, we could move to a bigger flat in Carnegie. I now had my licence and experienced the freedom of going and doing what I wanted.

I'd managed to get a decent job in the banking industry and lived for the weekends. I still hadn't really found the thing that floated my boat with horses but I was working with Starbuck and occasionally helping others out with their horses. The help, education, information, skills – or whatever you want to call it – were still out of reach and I found I was seeking knowledge but what I was finding just didn't gel with me.

I decided it was time to get back out there with Starbuck to find what else we could do, as I didn't feel challenged with just us.

It was a chance meeting with a physiotherapist that changed my life. I had lots of pain in my wrist from tendonitis caused by the repetition of my work, so I went to him looking for relief. We got to talking one day about horses. He raved about a woman he had started to see for dressage, and it all sounded amazing. Little did I know how agreeing to go to this five-day clinic would change my life and pathway again.

6

I found my religion

Off we went on a new adventure to open our minds to what else was out there. I convinced my sister Ruth to come with me for the five-day clinic. We hired a float and set out for our adventure. Ruth's horse Banjo was difficult to get into a float, so we had a friend help us. I watched and, although she got the job done, wasn't convinced we had just done the right thing, or that way of thinking about horse management sat with me well. *Be true to yourself kept just echoing in my mind.*

The five-day dressage clinic was held by a respected prior competitor. There were about 15 of us there with our horses. Most people there competed, but Ruth and I were just there to get out and be doing something. Over the five days, I did lots of lateral work and a lot of repetition.

Most horses complied with everything but there were no soreness checks and most horses by day three were starting to get quite cranky. Looking back, I would say most were now muscle-sore and starting to drop their backs and just bend their neck, but none of that detail was discussed.

We were told to look after our horses' backs by keeping them warm and that we needed to walk them out after concentrated work. One lady's horse must have been feeling the aches and pains more than the others and had a meltdown, where she threw the rider.

One of the other participants there was a Bowen and massage therapist for people and worked on the rider in the back of a float. They limped into the float and, sometime later, walked out. I then asked the lady who did the bodywork on humans whether she could check the horse. She told me she was learning to work the same with horses and this was way too much strain for horses to concentrate all into the five days.

We became friends with this lady – mainly because her horse lost the plot on day four, and she had a meltdown and felt she had just undone all the hard work and trust she had built with her horse over the years. As she sat crying, she looked at us and told us she wanted a beer.

Ruth drove off and came back with her wish. She walked up with the beer for her and said, 'You need this, and your horse will forgive you, no one is perfect, you are just trying to improve the both of you.'

I still think that lady from our first agistment taught me an amazing lesson – that you may not agree with how someone does something but look deeper into their intentions and what sits comfortably with you.

Day five was the sealer for me. I needed to understand and know more about biomechanics and how to condition your horse to cope in these situations or assess if this situation is even fair. The participant who arranged this instructor and the clinic was now part of a demonstration about to be given. She owned a spunky little mare that had her own attitude and didn't like constantly being pulled at. What they then did to this mare I will never forget, because it forged some strong ethics in me about what sort of equipment and training I am comfortable with and understand. None of what was done to that poor mare met the criteria.

This mare had a roller and bridle put on her, as well as tie-downs as sidelines. For those that don't understand what I am saying, this mare had a bridle on and a surcingle that was like a girth, but no saddle. It is like putting a belt around your horse's belly where the girth normally goes. From there, they clipped reins from the bit to rings on the side of the roller. They then proceeded to tighten the sidelines, forcing the mare to bend her neck otherwise it would become very painful in the mare's mouth, as the bit was pulling. Everyone could see how uncomfortable the mare was with this and she had now gone from scared to angry. She started jumping about, pinning her ears and they still wouldn't listen, it was upsetting to watch. I remember looking at her back. It wasn't rising but hollowing, the more they forced and tightened the sidelines. She now had two people wrestling with her.

Then it happened. The mare leapt multiple times, trying to fight off her containment. To me, it was obvious she was in pain and that this was never going to work. To be honest, it was extremely hard to watch. She squealed a deep, gut-wrenching noise multiple times, while she jumped and tried to throw herself on the ground when she still couldn't get relief.

The instructor's face was white and somehow managed to loosen one side, and so the mare immediately used the slack to relieve the torture from the bit and bent to the other side. They then released the remaining side. They then lunged this horse in circles on loose side reins, however the damage was done. The mare looked broken and, although grateful for the release, had learnt to fight pressure.

We heard later this horse was never right again and was sold or given away. She had issues with her back and neck. I found this all very distressing as I had never heard that terrifying squeal ever from a horse before and I imagined the pain she must have been feeling to have something mechanically inflict more pressure without release.

At the end of the five-day clinic, we were all just wanting to leave. As Banjo was the bigger horse, we went to put him on the float first. Go figure, he wasn't going to have a bar of getting in the float. Several people had gathered now and were giving us all types of advice. Ruth and I were happy just to use pressure and release for a try and take our time, everyone else thought it was some sort of race. Ruth knew Banjo better than anyone, and she kept saying, 'Don't push him past when he is trying, he gets scared and confused.' *Put so simply, but what some of us have searched our whole horse life to not only register but implement.*

The instructor of the clinic saw what was happening and offered her assistance. She said she had just been to a 'Bob' clinic (Bob was a worldwide trend of alternative training at that time) and said that, if she loaded our horse, he would never not load again. We watched as she swung a rope at him and then ran away from him. I had no idea what she was trying to do. She looked like she was scared and unsure of what she was doing. After some time, not only Ruth and I were losing faith, but so were the other people watching. The more confused the instructor got, the more worked up Banjo got. The instructor said it may take more time, but it is worth it. Ruth subtly advised she appreciated what the instructor was trying to do, but she understood she was a busy lady and that, after a five-day clinic, the last thing she expected her to do was load her problem horse, so we would take it from here.

Ten minutes later, once Banjo had calmed down, he was more than happy to get on the float when we re-introduced pressure and release for his try. There were some good things in this clinic, but by far the biggest thing I got out of it was that I must go watch this Bob guy, as I had heard he was amazing, and, instead, I felt like bagging the crap out of him.

Bob was still new to Australia back then and it was hard to get into one of his clinics. The only one I could see soon was one in New South Wales - I was in Victoria. It was a two-day horsemanship clinic and I had never seen any other clinics besides my last one. In the car, I went with a girlfriend I'd convinced to go with me, as I had to see what all the fuss was about for myself.

It started a bit too grand for me with music and a grand entrance after an introduction, and I was starting to think, *yep, wanker*. There was also one too many pretty women in the crowd that just looked besotted, and I was ready to leave. Then Bob came out. He began to talk and tell stories of how a horse thinks, and about how important a relationship was. I was beginning to get hooked because it all made perfect sense.

He then started working with some of the horses at the clinic and would explain what and why he was doing things. OMG ... finally. I found what had been missing the whole time. This made sense. This I could understand. It was like walking away from a car crash and watching a beautiful waltz. In reflection, every time over the last 12 years I replayed in my mind when things had gone amazingly with a horse and when it hadn't all now seemed crystal clear.

I started watching all of Bob's videos, reading his books, and attending any clinics I possibly could. I wanted to start doing his levels program with horses, with the thought of eventually instructing on his behalf. At one of these clinics I went to, I met a couple of other people with the same thoughts in mind. Bob promoted setting up a support group of like-minded people who wanted to follow his program, and so that is what I did.

There were 12 of us at the start and we called ourselves 'The Outriders'. We would take turns to organise an outing at an arena or someone's property, where we would meet for a day or weekend and spend the whole time working with ourselves and our horses. We were all quite different people but were all like-minded about the sort of methods and philosophy we were comfortable using with our horses. I loved this group. Everyone was so supportive, kind and happy to share their knowledge. We would set an agenda for the day of what exercises or training we would concentrate on, always ending with something fun or a competition among us just for 'shits and giggles'.

We travelled all over the place. From going to Narbethong, past the Black Spur, to the other side of Melbourne to Gisborne. We were all very dedicated and helped each other the best way we could. I started feeling that I was asking too much of Starbuck, so I put the word out I was looking for another horse. The new agistment property where we had moved Starbuck and Banjo to had a lot of horses on it. The man who ran the agistment, Don, also bred thoroughbreds for racing and knew a few stables where they had retired racehorses that wanted to be rehomed. I asked him to keep a lookout for any potential good horses that were cheap and sound for me to look at.

In the meantime, I was starting to get more confident with my newfound understanding of how a horse's mind works. I started working with other people's horses just for practice. Teaching horses basic ground manners, how to move their feet, do obstacles, float load, catch, work better with a rider on them, and, of course, liberty work. I found liberty work the most rewarding of everything I did.

The look in a horse's eye of complete trust, knowing they can run away, and you can do nothing about it. But, because of the communication and relationship you have set up, they choose to stay, watch your every move on the ground, or feel every movement and signal on their back, and just want to work with you. To this day, I still think it is one of the most amazing unions I have experienced. To have such a large animal, that is programmed to flee any danger and not trust predators, to willingly work with you and use all their agility and strength to carry you and protect you is just magical.

One day, Ruth allowed me to work with Banjo to finally sort out his floating issues. Don came out to watch. Banjo must have known I was on a bit of a mission and, accordingly, put on a show. To this day, and after float loading well over a hundred horses, I find most horses that have previous floating issues will comply to a point – and then demonstrate their fear or anxiety. Banjo did exactly that. The initial few steps were fine, but when we started to get to the nitty gritty of fully loading, he came out fighting. He tried rearing, dragging me off, hiding behind the breach doors and more.

Lucky for me, I was strong enough and confident enough now that I was more persistent – and, let's face it, stubborn and determined. *There are some advantages, sometimes, to being pig-headed.* Don watched as Banjo tried everything and, while watching the horse rear for about the fifth time, said, 'This will be interesting to see what happens,' and then walked away.

Banjo's heart rate was up, because of his anxiety and fear, and he looked at me as if to say, 'I trusted you, why are you doing this?'

We then came to what I see as the critical turning point. When you put pressure on and, no matter what happens or where you end up, you stay smooth and consistent until you get the one step forward, THEN GIVE … *I think since that day, and until now, I have quoted this hundreds of thousands of times, and, yes, all my current clients are probably laughing their heads off at how often I will push this point. Even when they don't want to hear it.*

I then left Banjo for five minutes standing there to think. He calmed down, relaxed his breath and dropped his head a little. He still wasn't certain of what he had done to get me to back off. I then asked, with the softest of pressure, for a forward step. He was as light as a feather. I stopped again and let him be for a minute. He looked at me as if to say, 'Okay, I get it, but that box is still in front of me'. We then walked in the float. He stopped halfway to question the pressure ever so lightly, I held firm, and, in a split-second, he came forward where I released all pressure and let him JUST BE. *Yes! Another saying I frequently belt out to clients still.*

I backed him out of the float, where he yawned so much, he almost fell over with his emotional and physical let-down. From that moment on, he loaded softly, slowly, and respectfully – every time. Don had just been watching the last time I loaded him and said, 'Well, I'm impressed. I thought you had no chance of ever getting that horse on the float.' It had taken me about 40 minutes, and I had never seen Banjo so relaxed and happy to work with me. It was extremely rewarding. Don offered me free agistment from then on if I would work with his thoroughbreds before they would go to the trainers. I worked with foals and yearlings, so they were easy to catch, lead, do their feet and float load.

***

Go figure, I was starting to get cocky. Thinking I could manage and train any horse. I started going to strangers' properties for free and sorting their floating issues. Then I met my match. I showed up at a property where the owner bred warmbloods. She had a four-year-old, unhandled stallion who was locked in a stable – and she wanted to show him. He was halter-broken to a point but was so strong and oblivious to any pressure. I should have walked away when I saw two guys go into the stable with a cane stick, a halter and lead, and fear in their eyes. That good old stubborn trait of mine - *not always a good thing* - kicked in and I took the horse by the lead.

I worked with him for two hours and barely got anywhere. I was physically and mentally questioning everything. I then thought logically and told the owner this was not going to get fixed today. The horse needed a lot of work and floating *wasn't* the issue but someone had made it that.

The horse could barely lead, had no respect, and was completely shut down. He needed a lot of groundwork first before involving a float – and she needed a professional. She didn't even thank me for my efforts. As I drove off, I thought, *what was I thinking?* He was a stallion; I was so naïve and stupid to think I was at this level. I was lucky I wasn't killed, and it was obvious the owner wouldn't have cared if I had been. I backed off doing free jobs from then, but also decided to learn more and respect myself a hell of a lot more.

I continued to work with Don's yearlings until they were about to turn two. I managed to get all four calm, relaxed, very eager to please and cooperative for anything asked softly. They were all great with their feet, leading, doing ground obstacle courses – and they were absolute angels to float load.

The day came when I was to hand them back and the racehorse trainer was to take them and start his training. When he came with the horse float to collect the first two horses, I tried to explain the method I had used and how they were extremely confident with pressure and release. All he did was laugh at me and say, 'I will take it from here.'

This trainer was not interested in what I had done, how, what these horses were used to and, to be perfectly honest, treated me like scum. He then grabbed the most sensitive of the four with incredible force and started to try to drag him on the float. This gelding complied with the first bit, but when he tried to come more forward so that the pressure was less, the poor horse received a smack from the handler. They then tried dragging him again instead of just gently asking him. I then understood they were not used to such willing horses and assumed this was the only way.

I protested when I saw the gelding start to baulk and get frightened with this new type of handling. Don was watching the whole time and I know it wasn't part of the deal, but I yelled 'Way too much force, just let me show you.' Both men looked at me like I was a piece of crap. I ignored their looks, grabbed the gelding and reset his try with the halter. He was nervous but as soon as I applied some gentler pressure, I felt him try and release, then watched him walk straight into the float and stand calmly.

To my disgust, they slammed the breach door on him, then grabbed another haltered gelding and dragged him in. This boy could cope with more, so just obediently followed. They slammed the other breach door and closed the back. This trainer then muttered down his nose, 'stick to what you know.'

I started to cry, as it was so unnecessary to put so much pressure on these young ones when they were so easy. I left so I didn't have to watch the next two horses, which loaded fine.

The next day, when I went to the agistment, Don sent out his friend to tell me the deal was off. I had to start paying agistment again, no more training of his horses. I started looking for another agistment.

While looking for another agistment, I started working up the road from Don's with a local riding school. The owner was an interesting lady. Very controlling and very much into the show world. She had some good practices for safety, which I did enjoy. First-time riders would only go on a few horses and were always put in a rectangle laneway, where they purely walked in a loop while the instructor would walk in front and explain about hands, feet and balance. I did enjoy this experience of teaching straight riding, as I quickly worked out the power of liberty work, with you on the ground signalling with your body to assist the ever-so unskilled rider on the horse's back. Being a typical riding school that was taught to pull the reins to stop, kick to go, and bend the horse with the reins, I initially thought I was wasting my time. However, in hindsight, thinking about it now, this experience and opportunity was my first professional (paid) teaching job of people, so I was blessed that this lady gave me a go.

I worked there one day a week and taught the beginners and intermediate classes. The owner of the business was very trusting of me and would only come to watch once every few weeks to ensure that how I was teaching met her standards. After a couple of months, the owner trusted me enough to run the school while she went showing, which meant I would also teach the advanced group. This was great fun, as you could push things a bit more.

I was working full-time in the bank, plus Prahran Market on a Saturday – and now Sunday teaching. After three months, this workload was starting to affect other aspects of my life, as I was only ever working or riding. My response was to quit teaching.

Don had found a horse that he thought I would be interested in. Indiana was a five-year-old thoroughbred chestnut gelding who was no longer racing. He was 15.3hh and incredibly sweet but troubled.

I must have had my stupid hat on again. I went out to see him as I wanted to do my levels of horsemanship and our Outriders group was still a major focus. When I got there, I tried to put Indiana in a circle on the ground. His response was to either do nothing or rear. I then got on him and got the same response to trying to bend him. I was looking at a horse that couldn't be convinced to move his feet without becoming erratic and dangerous. So what did I do? Yep, bought him, of course! I started using horse chiropractors, acupuncturists,

Bowen therapists, deep tissue massage therapists, you name it. Some helped and I started being able to feel when things weren't right, and I needed professional help to deal with a horse's ailment or injury. Indy taught me that.

I started doing all the groundwork with Indy, as well as getting a vet to do acupuncture on him. He was diagnosed with sacroiliac joint issues, which I was told was common for retired racehorses. Because they work so hard before their skeletal structure is ready, as well as the weight on their back, their hips are usually one of the first places to show wear and tear.

The vet even carried a set of cleaned bones from a horse, showing what happens to the hip joint and how it had ground out some of the socket. I was devastated. He said that, in his view, there wouldn't be one thoroughbred without some sort of damage in this area if they had been trained for racing. I tried to manage his pain with treatments, exercises, and straight-line work as much as I knew how to.

Indy was constantly improving with bending, flexibility, and strength. His physique had changed from when I got him. I could now get him to calmly lunge, do obstacles, half pass, side pass, back up and generally place his feet wherever I wanted. He was also starting to use his back more and engage when riding.

I had him doing lovely flat work at walk, trot, and canter. I still had two main problems though. He would get sore with lateral work and the vet advised, due to his pelvis damage, that this would always be the case and he would be better used just for straight bush riding. I rode Indy for several months, mainly in the bush, and minimised the lateral work I needed to do to achieve my horsemanship levels.

The other problem I was still having with Indy was the fact that, when he was cantering out on a trail, he would slowly but surely return to the racetrack in his mind and would want to flat-out gallop. I tried several things I had previously tried with other horses to check them and slow them down and none of this worked with him. I then spoke to my farrier, who did a lot of mountain bush racing, and he gave me the suggestion to take Indy to the other side of the agistment where there was a huge paddock with one ginormous hill and canter him in a massive loop on the face of the hill. When he would try to speed up, try to check him back. If he didn't check back, push him on. He explained that I should do this repeatedly until Indy wanted to slow down – and that then I should push him. Then try again and ask him to slow down and, when he does, quit. Repeat daily until he learns that, when you check him back, he should listen – otherwise he may get pushed more than what he bargained for. I was hesitant because I wasn't sure if I was a good enough rider, or if this was fair to the horse. This would make him blow excessively, and his lungs would have trouble getting enough air, causing stress ulcers and overexerted muscles. Quite simply, we were assuming Indy would be logical and not run himself into the ground.

I was still debating all the ethics of this method in my head when I heard there had been a car accident out on the road in front of our agistment because one of the girls' horses had bolted and she could not stop. I had worked on one-rein stops and disengaging Indy, but due to his pelvis issue, tight bends did cause him problems. This method doesn't work once your horse has momentum in a fast canter or gallop. I then felt I had a responsibility to sort this out. I was looking at trying to sell Indy to buy another horse that physically could handle lateral work. I would never want to put a horse out into the public where I would question whether they were safe as a riding horse.

I then picked a day and decided it was the right thing to do for both of us.

It was a mild day with a light breeze, as I didn't want it to be hot or raining because I was already feeling a bit of guilt at the possible outcome. I thought that, if the temperature was high, Indy would get hot too quickly and would make the situation even more dangerous. I didn't want it raining either, as I wanted the ground surface safe and not slippery.

I did some light groundwork first and kept telling Indy to catch on, as I didn't want to do the marathon ride. I was hoping that, subconsciously, he understood. I then did some gentle flat work under saddle and then rode him to the top of the hill.

I marked out our racetrack in my mind. I started at a walk, then a trot where, as usual, Indy was a soft, beautiful gentleman. We then began our canter. As Indy had so many other times when out of an arena situation, his canter was starting to build. I tried to check him back, sit back and deep, and ask with my hands, but he just kept trying to power on. I then said to myself, 'Okay, time to commit.'

This time, instead of fighting, I let him go. Man, oh man – did he think it was Christmas! The power and speed came on like a locomotive. I had to keep telling myself he can't do this forever, he will have to get tired eventually. We did a full lap of our mentally marked-out track and he was now starting to get into a good rhythm. I had never been on an ex-racehorse where I had said 'Okay, show me what you've got.'

Wow, thoroughbreds know how to gallop.

On our second lap, I tried again to check Indy back, but not a chance, so we kept going. I almost think Indy had got faster again now that he had settled into the loop and the initial excitement was starting to wane. His breathing was in a strong, even rhythm and was like music with the thunder of his hooves.

Third lap, I asked again for Indy to check back, but still nothing but a strong pull. We kept going. I was starting to think the danger of me coming off was gone now that the first burst of excitement had calmed, but now I was wondering if he would *ever* give up or if I was going to hurt, or possibly even kill him.

I checked again, and there was a slight try to slow down, but then he powered on. We had come this far, I felt that if I didn't continue, I would have made the problem worse. Just like when you desensitise a horse from something that is worrying them and, rather than continuing until they are relaxed, you quit while they are still scared and trying to escape. That never ends well.

Coming into the fifth lap, he started to slow without me asking. So, with tears in my eyes from the wind we had created with our speed, I asked him on. Indy was almost in shock, I think, but he picked up the pace.

I waited for a bit and asked him to check back. Nothing. I asked him on. After half a lap he slowed again. Now my tears were flowing from me questioning myself on whether this was the right thing to do. But I pushed him on.

What must be going through his head? Indy must be thinking 'WTF? They always wanted me to run when they let me go. Now they don't?'

A quarter of a lap on and I asked him to check back, it must have been more than a dozen times I had tried so far on our ride. This time he slowed. I relaxed the reins and just rubbed his neck and told him how good he was. We stopped and with Indy and me both sweating and blowing I jumped off and walked him back to wash him down. I think my legs were shaking more than his. Now I hoped the penny had dropped and physically he was ok.

The next day, we did the same routine with half the groundwork. This time, Indy still sped up when he went to canter but it wasn't frantic like the previous day. It took half the time and effort from the previous day to get an even better result. I was hopeful.

On the third day, we just rode our warm-up and then went to our track. I went into a canter, and I felt Indy hesitate. I made a few strides and asked him to check back, and he stopped. I burst out crying with joy and jumped off. I gave him a good ten minutes, then jumped back on. Indy now waited on me in the canter. If he did go to speed up and I checked him, he would bring himself down to maintain his current cadence and speed, or if I requested him to slow down. I was so proud of him. He was a bloody nice horse, with previous issues that were put on him.

I hoped in some sort of way he understood why I did what I did. I know he was now definitely calmer and more relaxed, so I felt he did on some level.

***

I took Indy to several Outriders' meetings until he became the reliable one who just couldn't physically do what I currently wanted. I will never forget one meeting where we had a great giggle – or at least the group did while hanging it on me.

We would set up obstacle courses and then do them one by one while everyone else in the group watched.

Indiana during training

Then, at the end, those watching would give feedback. It was a great, safe environment in which to be honest with each other. I was trying to canter Indy over a small jump and every time I got to the base of the jump he would stop. He wasn't refusing or avoiding – he would just calmly stop. It was late in the day and the rest of the group had started on the beers and wine and were quite amused by this and in fits of laughter.

The group asked me to do it again and, sure enough, Indy would stop just at the base of the jump, beautifully relaxed. To this, my audience was in fits of laughter, to the point where one of them fell off the fence they were sitting on. After three attempts, I protested that I wasn't trying again until they told me what the hell was going on. In unison, they all said, 'Look where you want to go.' Sure enough, I had been looking down at the base of the jump each time, without even realising. I had got Indy so good and responsive that he thought he was doing the right thing. With that, I went to do the jump a fourth time while giggling, looking up and screaming 'Is this better?' Straight over without hesitation and smooth as a baby's bum.

That one incident has stuck in my mind and made me so aware of others and my focus – more than anything else anyone has ever said to me. I couldn't afford another horse, so, as much as I hated the thought of it, I put Indiana up for sale. I thought I wouldn't get much interest, as I was brutal in my advertisement, saying 'trail riding only, not suitable for eventing or dressage'.

I had several people come and have a look and a ride of Indy. Some were okay, some were just flat-out rude and didn't listen or respect what I was saying about how to work with him and what he was suited for.

I got to the point where I told one woman to get off him as he was not for sale to her. She told me she would buy him and sort out his issues while she pushed and pulled on him and tried to explain to me that once she put tie downs on him and a martingale on him, she would get him right. I had to hold myself back from running at her and attacking her. Instead, I told her mum, who was standing next to me, that she better get her daughter off my horse before I go nuts.

A few days later, I had a call from a lady who I instantly bonded with. We spoke for two hours on the phone before I agreed she should come to meet him. She had just lost her previous horse, who had always had floating issues and was nervous about trucks. She wanted a trail riding horse for the bush. She said she didn't care if he got a little pumped with the canter, as she was confident if he was good with large vehicles and was good at floating.

I was very excited about this lady coming to try Indiana, as I felt we were on the same page with our thoughts on horses. The day she came, she brought a float to check out if he would load and or buy him and take him home. She ran her hands over Indy and did a couple of exercises with him on the ground. She then did some flat work with him in a flat paddock and was lovely and gentle with him. You could see she was a confident rider as she took him through his paces at a walk, trot, then canter. He looked very relaxed, smooth, and happy with this lady; I was hoping that she was keen. That's when she announced he was sold if she could ride him with traffic and if he float-loaded. I had left Don's and was at another local agistment in the area. This agistment had a two-lane bitumen road that was slow but constant with traffic at the entrance of the driveway. There was only a small narrow gravel walking track on the side barely big enough for a horse. This went for about 200 metres before you could turn left down a gravel side road, which was safer for a trail. I still had Starbuck, so I quickly grabbed him and jumped on bareback, with halter and lead, so I could ride out with this lady and Indiana in case something went wrong. Just as we were about to ride out the driveway from the agistment property I could see and hear a rather large truck coming down the road. Before I could say anything, this lady rode Indiana straight out the driveway, turned left at the road and rode him on the white line edging the bitumen from the gravel. I had hoped she had looked to make sure no other traffic was coming from the other side of the road, as the truck had to move slightly across the lane to not run them over. I was about to yell at her that this horse was not hers yet and that what she just did was incredibly dangerous when she turned her head with the biggest smile on her face as Indiana did not blink or move an inch in his relaxed walk stride.

She yelled in an over-excited voice. 'He is amazing, I love him. Sold!'

We continued to ride a little further and then turned around and went back to the agistment. This lady was delirious, she was so happy. She then proceeded to show me the new wardrobe she had just bought for him (she said her gut feeling on the phone was that he was the one). Full new set of floating boots, and two new rugs that we tried on and fit perfectly.

The last requirement was that he float loaded. This, I knew, wasn't going to be an issue. The only issue was explaining to her how he had been trained. As I tried to explain to her how to just drive him in gently while we stood at the float and she held Indy, she mimicked me while looking at me and Indy just loaded gently. She then turned to look at Indy and he was already completely in the float relaxed and ready to go.

This lady was a sook like me and just started crying. She was so pleased. I had done the whole full disclosure of the reason I was selling him; and gave her the details of the vet I had used and what he had said. Then watched them drive away. I was sad, but happy I had found his perfect next home for where he was at.

Indiana's new owner rang me a month later. She had been riding him and floating him weekly to Bunjip State Park where there were several horse trails and he had not put a foot wrong. Whether she rode him by himself or with a group. Her girlfriends had asked if I had any more horses like this as he was their perfect horse as well. She explained how, even if he did get a little excited, he would look magnificent but would behave perfectly and was the best riding horse she had been on. She promised me she would never sell him; he was with her for life. I was so pleased for them both. The last thing she said before she left was that she had a vet check done on him and her vet advised he would pass and there was nothing wrong. I was even more pleased for her. Physically, he couldn't cope at the stage where he was to manage the type of work I needed but was perfect for this lady's needs. She couldn't get better than that.

7

Matilda

I was 21. My boyfriend, Tom, and I were still together and had bought and moved into our first home in Upper Ferntree Gully. It was an 11-square Western Red Cedar split-level home on the side of a hill – but a mansion in my eyes. We got married just before my 22nd birthday and life was full of hope, joy and challenges. I felt the world was my oyster. I felt incredibly safe and was living the life I wanted. I was still working full-time in the banking industry but was now in foreign exchange, which is totally different to branch banking. I commuted to the city every day and was learning very much how the corporate world worked. I was extremely focused on learning and experiencing more with horses and was still running the Outriders group.

I wanted to start my own horse under saddle. A horse that had not been physically or mentally abused by anyone had the most potential for being sound and fit for the journey I was planning for the two of us.

I started doing a bit more research on certain breeds and going to watch shows and performance days. I can't even remember what the event was that I attended - *got to love becoming middle-aged and the old memory going* - but they were demonstrating all the different breeds of horses. Each breed came out and did a demonstration of what they were well-known and recognised for. Every breed that came out was very specific to what their skills were used for and about now I was thinking that I just needed a younger, taller Starbuck who, technically was a mongrel, but was versatile.

Then the Australian Stock Horse (ASH) Society came out, with their claim of the versatile horse. I liked their confirmation and background to the breeding of mixing thoroughbred horses with other more robust breeds. The first two horses came out cutting a couple of calves and were full-on herding and driving. They then left the yard and out came another two ASHs, one doing some beautiful dressage movements, while the other did show-jumping. I was more than impressed. Then, to further blow my mind, the original first two ASHs came back out driving a cart. They were superb. It was everything I wanted in a horse.

Brains, work ethic, character, physical ability, and a nature to be so flexible and just work at what you apply them to.

Finally, the second set of two ASHs came back in. Instead of doing dressage and show-jumping, one was now standing at liberty on a box, while the other did trot circles around them, again at liberty. I was sold. This was the breed for me and what I wanted in a relationship with my next horse.

I started doing some research and looking for any ASH for sale, but for anything unstarted, they were very young, and I would have to wait several years before I could start work on their back. I have strong views on when a horse should first experience the weight of a rider on their back, and to what age it is appropriate to ride for any length of time. As I was educating myself on the biomechanics of horses, the skeletal structures and the age they developed, I didn't and don't support getting on a horse too young. *Please don't nail me to a cross for my beliefs. We are all different and I was and am learning to be true to myself.*

I believe no horse should have any weight of a rider on them until a rising four-year-old, and no riding past an occasional walk until a rising five-year-old. This, of course, differs on breed, environment, and where the individual horse is at for its body and mind. I started ringing every ASH stud in Victoria, asking what the youngest horse they had for sale unstarted. I must have rung over half a dozen studs where every answer was rising two-year-old or two-and-a-half-year-old until one of the stud managers asked what I wanted the horse for. I explained that I wanted to start my own horse but didn't believe in starting them under saddle until they were a rising five-year-old and I didn't want to have to wait. He straight away said, 'You want to speak to Gail, she is your type of person.'

I then rang the number for Gail who had her own ASH stud. Gail abruptly answered the phone, and I explained why I was calling. I then proceeded to go through what I felt was like a two-hour interview on the phone before she would even let me know where her stud was. Gail finally expressed I sounded okay, and that she was okay for me to come have a look at three she had for sale. A five-year-old, seven-year-old and eight-year-old, and all had been haltered and floated but never started for riding. Her stud was two and a half hours from home, so I decided to take a float in case I liked any. *I was on a mission.*

We arrived at the stud the following weekend and all I remember was driving down the driveway to see a magnificent black colt in one of the paddocks strutting around and rearing to show his presence. He was majestic. We arrived at the house to a very welcoming Gail. She showed us around the property a little and explained each horse before we saw them. I asked to see the five-year-old mare first, as the others were getting a little old to start under the saddle – even for me.

We walked down to a paddock with a grey and chestnut mare with a white blaze. She explained the chestnut had floated a few times and her daughter had qualified her for the Royal Melbourne Show lead class. On the morning of the show, she startled and cut below her fetlock on the float ramp. Nothing serious but enough that it was bleeding a bit so needed bandaging - *lucky for me horses aren't accepted in the show ring with a bandage* - so that ended her show prospects for that day, where they were planning on selling her. That was two years ago. Gail's daughter did all the horse handling and starting but, due to family, had stopped soon after that day. This mare had not had any handling since, except worming.

I asked Gail if I could go into the paddock to catch her. 'Good luck,' Gail laughed.

I entered the paddock and with that, the mare ran flat out into the corner of the paddock and spun a 360-degree turn and leapt forward into a strong collected canter. This mare was so special that she could move like that. This was the best moving and sound horse I had seen in a while.

I turned to Gail and said, 'Sold!' Gail was in shock and didn't understand how I was willing to buy this mare without touching her and the fact she was running away from me. I told her, 'All I can see is her movement and it is stunning.'

If she hadn't been handled for two years, she had every right to run from a stranger.

I worked at liberty with the mare and caught her within five minutes. She was very much in paddock condition, with a scruffy coat, big belly, rough hooves, and sensitive muscles. I worked with her a little and could tell immediately how smart and willing she was – she just needed to trust me. She was probably the most sensitive horse I had come across to date and I loved it.

Gail was so honest about everything, I wasn't concerned and felt I had just won the lottery with my perfect horse for $500, which back then was a very cheap price for this type of horse.

I worked a little more with her and then loaded her on the float to take home. Just as we were leaving, Gail asked if I was interested in the black colt in the front paddock. He was a two-year-old and only offered for sale to me and one other person.

I told her it was a dream of mine to own a property, breed horses and bring them up our way but added that I didn't have the property yet and I didn't have the skills for a colt or stallion. When she said she would wait until I was ready and told me to stay in contact, I replied by laughing.

***

Ruth and I now had another agistment property where it was just our horses, which was great from a feed and property management side of things. I was still running the Outriders and started dragging my new mare I'd renamed Matilda to every meeting we had. I was starting to bond with her. We would spend countless hours playing at liberty amongst the trees in a bush part of the agistment and I couldn't ever imagine anything ever going wrong between us. I still rode Starbuck in between but he was enjoying not being pushed so hard now he was in his mid-teens.

Matilda was the first horse I'd ever started for riding – and I did it by myself. I was 25 years old. Everything seemed incredibly easy during the first few rides, as we had such good communication and language happening on the ground. I felt I had another feather in my cap, but reality was about to remind me how inexperienced I really was.

It was maybe our third or fourth ride when Matilda just stopped. Without thinking about her and where she was at – just needing reassurance – I kicked her with both feet. That mistake taught me an important lesson.

I had a super sensitive mare that I had created to be push-button, but then I slammed a button when she was unsure. She threw a massive buck. We were on the side of a hill, and although I would always curl to the left, thinking I would come off the near left side, due to the hill, I went over onto the right. With me curled to the other side, my right shoulder hit the ground from a decent height and took the full impact. I was screaming in pain. Ruth drove her Gemini into the paddock to get me to the hospital while I was crying to just let me get back on.

'I don't want to wreck my horse.' Ruth very kindly bullied me into the car and let Matilda go. *Thanks, Ruth.*

When we arrived at the hospital and they were taking my medical history, they said, 'Great, another horse accident.' Must have been a busy day in emergency! My shoulder didn't look like it was where it was supposed to be. The doctor was guessing dislocation. However, after the x-rays, I was told it was soft tissue damage only, with no need for surgery, just a sling for a while. I can't remember how long it took to heal. All I was thinking about was how frightened Matilda was and I must restore her trust. This is when I really worked on idling a horse up. Teaching them when you climb up on something to move into a position where you can mount. To be safe, I made sure she was relaxed and her feet - *yes, I give horses human parts* - felt like cement on the ground and didn't move. I then worked on the forward again and instead of pushing her hard, like an educated horse could cope with, when she became unsure, I would go back to reassuring her and only pushing to get a little try, instead of expecting a massive change. *Matilda taught me feel.*

***

We continued to improve and go to our weekends away with the Outriders. It was now that I wrote in a scrapbook (and put it hidden in my cupboard) what my dream job would be: a job where I worked with people and horses to get them working together and be able to train, educate and work out their problems. *Little did I know, when I found this scrapbook 21 years later, the apprenticeship I had undertaken.*

I also was starting Bob's training program. I had Matilda now cantering up to me when I climbed a fence or ladder at liberty so I could get on her back. I started riding her only with a string around her neck. I could side pass her at liberty. Load her on the float forwards, backwards, from me sitting on a chair and at liberty. I felt I had made up for my previous stuff-up when starting her. Then things began to change. Matilda started getting a bit cinchy - *not wanting her saddle done up* - not so keen to be with me and got sore in the back whenever I rode. This would lead me to two years and spending thousands on vets, chiropractors, and bodyworkers, all of whom could not fix her.

I then had a horse friend question her diet. She explained the whole of the Yarra Valley was Selenium deficient and that over time this can cause horses to 'tie up', which was the symptoms Matilda displayed. So, instead of getting blood tests, this friend suggested we do our own clinical trial and give her a Selenium supplement and see if it improves in six weeks. The product I bought cost $35 for a tin, which I added to her feed and covered her for eight weeks. Seriously, I had spent probably well over $2500 in the last two years trying to work this out, let alone the damage I felt it was doing to us. Matilda was sometimes so sore I couldn't ride her. Well, after a few weeks, slowly but surely, Matilda got better and within six weeks was back to her best. I was dumbfounded and vowed I needed to educate myself better.

At the same time, things were not going so great in my work life. I didn't like the corporate world. The industry I was in was very competitive. I had experienced multiple incidents of sexual harassment, intimidation, and bullying. The work environment back in the 90s was very different to now. I also was experiencing tendonitis from poor workstation set-up and fast, stressful computer use. I covered all my own costs and never asked work for anything. The only time I did speak to management about possible work cover was when I needed surgery for a third ganglion that appeared on my wrist – as big as a golf ball and quite painful. I needed plastic surgery to remove it because of where it was, and the damage done to the tendon.

I had just verbally received a promotion at work in front of 30-odd staff and felt that work should be willing to work with me to cover some of the costs. Boy, was I wrong. As soon as I put the work care claim in, my promotion was pulled. I was put

Matilda at Ben Clinic

into another job, but honestly, my heart and loyalty were gone to this company, so after 12 months or so I left.

I was blessed that my husband supported me in this, and as he was now earning a good income, I could try something else for a while. I applied for a position at Glenormiston College to do an Advanced Diploma in Horse Management by correspondence. I got in and I was in my element with learning everything, I loved it. I also started working part-time for an agency, back to branch banking, so that I was still earning some money.

I felt so blessed to be able to study and work part-time, while still working constantly with my horses.

8

Education and clinic junkie

I remember this part of my life very fondly. I had contemplated going back to school and getting my VCE, so I could apply for Veterinary Science but, in short, we had a mortgage and horses to pay for and, even if we didn't have kids, we were looking at another ten years before I would be earning money again. So, I did what I thought was the next best thing, working part-time while studying and doing my horse work on the side.

I loved studying by correspondence. Pasture, water, feed management, anatomy, common diseases, property management, and more – but did miss the contact with like-minded people.

My favourite subject was one of the property management ones. There were five in total. For one of them, there was an opportunity to go as a group for two weeks and travel through Scone in NSW to visit 30-odd horse studs. This was amazing. We got to go into some of the best horse studs in Australia and go behind the scenes.

It was a gift to be able to trundle through 30 different properties and see the facilities, their goals, and how they managed their horses. We had to write a comparative case study for this subject on two of the studs. I chose a thoroughbred breeding stud that had been in the one family for three generations and was nestled within a valley on thousands of acres. The land was amazing, and the stud was one of the first to work out that over-fat mares during pregnancy caused greater birthing difficulties. The management of these mares they put in place to change the outcome of better and healthier birthing rates and foals was so simple but brilliant.

The other stud I used for my case study was an inner Sydney Arab breeding stud for show horses. They only owned 20 acres and leased another 20 acres a short drive away. The learnings from this stud were just as interesting – about how to make things work on limited land. I was pretty much in my element and was now daydreaming about our own property and breeding program.

Two other subjects I needed to attend the university for were Breeding and Breaking and Training.

Both entailed a week at the university, which was about a four-hour drive away. The breeding subject opened my eyes to how stallions could behave when treated a certain way. The experience of watching and being part of breeding horses was invaluable. To do the theory of mare's cycles but then to see again and again the behaviour just cemented our learnings. It showed me a lot about the industry and what I was and wasn't comfortable doing. *Be true to yourself and what you believe but educate yourself first before you bag anyone or anything out. Even then, just because it's not what you agree with, doesn't mean it is wrong.*

The breaking and training I did later, and boy was that interesting. I had full-on arguments with my lecturer. Again, I learnt what I didn't feel comfortable with and what sort of trainer I wanted to be.

We were paired up with other students and, in short, the horse we were given they had tried to start three times. We were told she still bucked when starting each time, so we better stay focused. *Well, that doesn't sound right.* The lady I was working with had a baby at home and was stressed she was going to get hurt, so I offered to ride first. We had been lunging the mare as requested with the saddle on and it was now time to get on. Hobbles were put around their front legs - a bit like leather handcuffs - so the mare had to stand still, then you got on and they took off the hobbles. Go figure, the mare bucked out on me until I came off and hit the round metal yard wall. Cut my finger which was bleeding, but the words coming out of my mouth to the lecturer were more toxic. I got pulled away into a room and bandaged and pretty much told that this is an industry, and that, the way I was talking, no one would make money. *Which I can now see, but don't necessarily agree with – it takes more time to do things differently. It's just a different way. I think you need to take the time it takes, but the industry back then didn't pander to this. Thankfully, times have changed. My mindset and experience have now also taught me that, in the long run, it doesn't take more time. Laying great foundations takes time but pays off with everything you do. The real issue for me was that I was only comfortable with asking things physically and mentally of the horse when appropriate.*

My lecturer was doing 'tough love'. Again, in her mind and her position, she was responsible for getting me ready to work in the industry, and she did. She created a rebel. Thank you.

I also used this time to get as much practical education on training as I could. I attended lots of horsemanship clinics, including Wayne Banney, David Stuart, Ray Hunt and Buck Brannaman. One of the biggest things that I learnt from watching all these amazing men with horses was to watch what the horses thought of them. The men I respected the most were the ones that I thought I could learn the most from – and, in my eyes, were great horsemen.

I noticed a similar pattern of behaviour every time they handled a client's horse. I noticed whenever one of them grabbed a participant's horse to work with it and then handed them back, as the clinician walked away, the horses' eyes would follow. The horse would watch them leave with a softness, respect and almost longing to be with them. It was the first time they were really understood. It reminded me of when, in a movie two people meet for the first time and have the best conversation and understanding within a few minutes, more than anyone else they have met in their life. Almost like love at first sight. *I always say to clients now that if you watch a clinician, watch what the horse does in this circumstance. If the horse doesn't stare at them like they have just met the love of their life, I would question what you could learn of this person if the horse doesn't think that much. Let alone, if the horse watches them go in fear.*

I remember booking into a clinic, which was held in NSW. The horseman running it was an amazing man from the USA, Ray Hunt. There was Colt starting - *it's really starting any horse, it's just called that* - and horsemanship clinic. I had booked in for the five days with Matilda doing horsemanship; I was very excited. The week before the clinic, I got a call to say there wasn't enough interest in the horsemanship part of the clinic so it wouldn't be running. I was disappointed but still, I went to watch it anyway. I don't agree with everything but man, what a breath of fresh air. This guy was amazing. From being strongly influenced by a type of pyramid-style training with natural horsemanship, this cowboy just blew the shackles off. I watched as he showed three different ways to load a horse on a float but used the same basic horsemanship principles but was customising to where the horse was at. This was the next level. The thing I most respected Ray for was there was no bullshit. No marketing, no hidden agenda, just there for the horse. Don't get me wrong, he crushed several people's egos, but the drive he had to do the right thing by the horse was poetry to watch.

In later years, when Ray had passed, it shocked me to see the enormous following it created. I always find that confusing

– how people are kinder and more appreciative of what you have to offer when you can't anymore. Amazing how time and mortality change everything, considering Ray is now seen by many as one of the best horsemen to ever share their knowledge. It's like someone ending a relationship because they're always thinking there is a greener pasture, but then realise what they had. I love the saying, 'You don't know what you have until it's gone'.

This is very much my mantra these days. With all aspects of life, enjoy the moment. Things may, and can, change in the blink of an eye.

I read somewhere on Ray's Facebook page that his favourite poem was 'Man in the Mirror'. I read it and loved it. I wish that before any person was allowed to touch a horse or human, they would have to read this poem first.

'The Guy in the Glass Poem (The Man in the Mirror)'

When you get what you want in your struggle for self,
And the world makes you king for a day,
Then go to the mirror and look at yourself,
And see what that man has to say.

For it isn't a man's father, mother or wife,
Whose judgement upon him must pass,
The fellow whose verdict counts most in life,
Is the man staring back from the glass.

He's the fellow to please, never mind all the rest,
For he's with you clear to the end,
And you've passed your most dangerous, difficult test,
If the man in the glass is your friend.

You can fool the whole world down the pathway of years,
And get pats on the back as you pass,
But the final reward will be heartache and tears,
If you've cheated the man in the glass.

Dale Winbrow was first published in *The American Magazine* in 1934.

An interesting thing about this poem is that the initial version I saw was written as Anonymous, supposedly found written in a death row cell of a prison - *it could have been, and they just didn't know the author.* Various people spun it off as their own and there are a couple of word changes and several different titles in different versions. However, after investigation, the correct author is Dale Winbrow. Human nature, hey. If you read and understand the words and meaning of the poem, how could you spin it off as your own? Some people never seem to stop disappointing me.

***

I continued to run the Outriders group and learnt so much from these amazing people within the group, but also all the other horsemen they encouraged me to go see. This was a great time of life for me. I stopped going to Bob's clinics and being a member, and stopped doing my training with him. I was halfway through my second part in his program and just found this was becoming too structured and not the way I wanted to go.

I am forever thankful for everything I learned and for opening my eyes, but I had now seen a lot of other trainers and was developing methods that I was comfortable with and looked at the whole training thing as relationship, communication, and a language.

The Outriders was great for showing this. One of the members suggested we invite this up-and-coming young man who was gifted with horses to do private clinics with our group on the weekends we meet. This young man was Ben. This tall skinny lad *(sorry, Ben)* was one of the most talented men I had seen with a horse for his age. He had a lot to offer and taught us all an incredible amount over the next few years.

***

Another incident I fondly remember with the Outriders was a weekend when Sharon, one of the ladies in the group, and I hired a float for one of the meetings that was being held in Gisborne. Sharon and I had been spending a lot of time together with our horses and had a great relationship. Sharon's horse had a few floating issues we had been working on and was now at a pretty good stage of confidence, but we still tried to go to meetings together for company, confidence and to save money.

This day, when we picked up the float, it was probably not the best float we had hired, but we were assured by the owner it was safe. So, we hooked it on, and I went and picked up Matilda then went to Sharon's to pick up her horse. We were enjoying the trip across town laughing and acknowledging how far we had come with our horses when we heard a bang. I felt the float drop on one side and stopped as carefully but quickly as possible. We were right out the front of Spencer St Station in Melbourne. Cars, trucks and trams going everywhere. We had a flat tyre on the float and needed to change it with the spare. Neither of us knew what to do - *I know it was shocking* - but I thought, I have Road Assist, so time to use them. We called Road Assist and they advised they would come and change the tyre, but the horses were not allowed to stay in the float for safety reasons. I did say I thought maybe it was safer for the horses to stay in a confined box because of where we were, but because of OHS (Occupational, Health and Safety rules), their attendant couldn't have live animals in the float. *I did wonder at the time, what would have happened if we were a truck carrying 100 sheep or something.*

We set up two hay nets with lucerne, thinking we needed to bring out the big guns to keep the horses happy while we waited for the Road Assist man. Once he arrived, we asked him to control the traffic while we unloaded the horses, which he did. They both came off calmly, even though Matilda took a very large step avoiding the floor closest to where the now damaged tyre was.

We tied the horses up in what was then a car park type of set-up at Spencer St station, across the footpath to the float. Both horses were not fussed at all and just munched on the lucerne hay as if to say, 'Wow, we must have done something right – they brought out the good stuff.'

I was freaking out and Sharon was as calm as a cucumber - *never understood this saying but assume it's because cucumbers smooth spicy food?* It was normally the opposite: Sharon freaking, while I was calm.

Sharon calmly asked, 'Do you want a coffee? I might go get us some coffee.'

My answer was pretty much 'WTF?' We then both burst into hysterical laughter. We had been so nervous about what could happen and something minor happened and the horses really didn't give a crap.

Once the man changed the float tyre, he then offered to stop the traffic again while we loaded our horses. This man knew nothing about horses, that was obvious. We didn't bother filling him in on our experiences previously with one of the horses or that the reliable one with floating, Matilda, just had a monstrous fright with something exploding under her feet. Sharon and I just looked at each other and acted as normal as we could, like this shit happens every day for our paddock horses and while this gentleman stopped traffic - being cars, trucks and one oncoming tram, we loaded our horses on.

I asked Matilda first, who now trusted me regardless of circumstances, and she gently and politely stepped up the ramp. Then she jumped where the wheel had been under her feet and landed in the perfect spot and lovingly turned softly to look at me as if to ask, 'Is this ok?'

I told her how amazing she was, she knew it in my voice. I was so grateful for such a beautiful soul. *Daggy as it sounds, this is my sort of competition, where you don't know what circumstances are going to be thrown at you, you can't pre-train for it directly, but because of everything you have done together, you are both winners.*

Sharon then asked her horse on, and he quietly cruised in next to Matilda. We closed the float up and thanked the gentleman from Road Assist, who had watched and held the traffic back for all of one minute for us both to load and lock everything up. The man said, 'Gee, it's good horses just get on like that, hey.'

Both Sharon and I both burst out laughing again telling him,' You have no idea how good it is.'

By the time we got to Gisborne, we were both ready for a sleep. It was now 11 am and we had run two hours late because of our incident, but we didn't care. In our eyes, all those hours of training and working with our horses just paid off. In our world, we had just climbed Mt Everest.

9

I have a dream Giyabwe

Time seems to speed up the older you get. After 18 months or so, I felt I needed to get back to full-time work. I managed to get a job with one of the new pay television companies popping up and started there as a cashier for sales representatives and technicians.

Being a new company and industry, things were very exciting and constantly changing. I moved into a minor management role quickly and the full-time hours I was working were closer to 50 or 60 hours a week rather than 38 hours a week. It was getting harder and harder to do my university study, and in recognition of the complexity of the course I was doing, when Melbourne University changed to have Glenormiston under their umbrella, the Diploma I was doing had now been reclassified as a Bachelor of Applied Science in Horse Management. This was great, but it also meant another three or four units of subject matter had been added.

I now had the dream of owning a horse property. Adding to my previous dream job description, I wanted to add breeding the perfect horse. I had now seen how much physical and emotional damage most horses carried by their previous circumstances and life that I wanted to breed our own where they would be blessed with the best possible upbringing I knew how to give.

From the best training and handling I could offer with my limited experience - *in my view and what I believed in* - to the best environment I could offer from paddocks, management, feed, etc. I thought if I could give them what I believed was the best opportunity physically and mentally, we would have some amazing horses. It was my dream to live my philosophy of what I believed with horses and educate others.

The years became a bit of a blur. The company I worked for had been bought over several times and was now one of the main players in telecommunications. I now worked in Melbourne CBD and was averaging about 70 hours a week working. I was now in a semi-senior management role and earning good money. Tom and I decided to look for our horse property. We found what we thought was perfect rather quickly but had put five offers in so far with no luck – we just couldn't stretch ourselves financially any further.

We looked at several other properties and nothing matched up. I thought if I held off having kids a few more years, even though I wanted them now, and kept working hard, we could do this. I was very lucky my husband was now earning a very decent wage, which made it easier when we went back a week later with our sixth and final offer. WE GOT IT. It was a six-month settlement and, although the timing of selling our first house meant we had to rent a very tiny house in between settlements, it was worth it.

In June 1998, we moved into our new home and property. I was 29 years old and never believed it was possible to be in this position. The property was in Macclesfield, Victoria, which is known for its high horse population to human ratio. It is situated between the Dandenong Ranges and the Yarra Valley. It was 20 acres, well set up with paddocks, and had a simple but nice 18-square farmhouse with a bullnose veranda. The driveway to the house was in the centre of the property and went for 100 metres to bring you to the heart of the property where the house was.

I thought I was the luckiest person in the world. I couldn't believe we could ever own such a beautiful property where I could create my dream. We named the property Giyabwe. Giyabwe means 'I had a dream' in one of the Native American languages. Navajo? Cherokee? I'm honestly not sure. The reason we chose this was because of the dream I wanted, and the Native Americans were the first ones I know of to work with their horses in the fashion I was attracted to. Liberty work and having a great relationship with their horse was built in their culture.

I was very lucky Tom continued to climb in his career and this allowed us to make improvements to the property. We both were working 60 to 70 hours a week on average and had to travel interstate at times. With all this going on, I stopped my studies and never finished my degree. I think I only had six or seven units to go. I regret this deeply. I wish I could have managed to go back and finish my degree as I feel I don't put myself first enough. It would have meant a tremendous amount to me to have completed this degree considering I was a high school dropout that left home at 17. But I felt I was being selfish and, with the property, I felt it was being about me a bit too much and what I wanted.

Also, when you are getting up every morning at five am to do horse feeds, travelling an hour and a half to get to work each way and getting home between seven to nine pm most nights to then do the horse feeds again and fall into bed by 10.30 pm, there is not too much time left in the day. If we were doing interstate work, typically either one of us would leave by three am and sometimes not get home till midnight on the day we would fly back.

One of the last things I did before leaving university, once we bought the property, was go back and buy the mare we tried to start at the university. I got her for my sister, Ruth, thinking that with good consistent training, she would come good and, if it didn't work out, she would make a great broodmare.

Without writing another novel within this novel, Ruth changed this mare's name to Tea, and she did a wonderful job with her, but she never became a reliable riding horse. I knew there was something wrong but didn't have the skills to work it out. We put it down to her having had too much damage previously either mentally or physically and that we weren't able to fix it. I took Tea back off Ruth as promised sometime later.

Matilda was still amazing and a joy. I was so busy working in the corporate world and then on weekends working on the property to try to keep on top of things that I stopped organising the Outriders group.

Sadly, no one else in the group at the time wanted to take on the responsibility, so we let the group finish. This group had run for eight years meeting every month on average. That is just under a hundred meetings. Wow, thank you to all of you. I was blessed to have been a part of such a great group. I wish we had had one last party or weekend away. What a great chapter in my life I spent with amazing people who shared a passionate belief in how we worked with our horses.

I started organising and holding clinics at our property for trainers I respected. I did this for several years and was blessed to have them come and share their knowledge. A big shout-out again to Ben, who did several clinics at our property and was a great influence on me.

It was at this time that Gail rang me and asked if I was ready for that black colt yet. OMG. Gail still said he was only available to me or one other person and the other person already had a colt and didn't want a second.

Was I skilled enough? We now had the property, and it was part of the dream. I rang Gail and asked if I could bring a great horseman with me to have a play and tell me whether I was being an idiot and what he thought of the horse and whether he thought he was a good stallion for our program. So, I rang Ben and asked if he was up for a road trip. Luckily, he said yes, and we decided again to take my new float with us, in case we liked him.

We showed up the following weekend and, as we entered the driveway, the black colt was now on the other side of the driveway, bigger, stronger, and more stunning in my eyes than ever.

Ben smiled as we drove past him and said, 'He doesn't look too bad.' His name was Java. He was now between 15.1hh and 15.2hh – a brown/black five-year-old. He was magnificent. He was unhandled, as far as he had only had the halter on a few times and Gail had someone lead him a little.

He was given worming pellets in his feed and had had no other work done with him. Ben went into the paddock to catch him, and he put on a beautiful display of his movement and character.

After a short time, Ben caught him and started doing a little ground handling with him, just getting control of his feet. After about 30 minutes, Ben led him over to me. I asked him what he thought, and the answer is something I will never forget. Ben smiled and said, 'If you don't want him, I'm taking him.'

With that, I bought Java.

Ben again showed his great skills with loading Java and travelling him back to our property. Ten minutes after leaving Gail's, I heard a rumble in the float. Java had got his head and neck on the wrong side of the divider, and it was causing him to get unbalanced. I asked Ben if we should unload him and load him back on. Ben responded, 'Not a chance.'

We were on the side of the road and the risk of something going wrong was too great. Ben tried to manipulate his head back, but it wasn't working. I started to get nervous, and Ben responded, 'He got himself in this, he can get himself out,' and with that, gave him a decent whack on the nose to frighten him. With that, Java bent his neck more and got his head back the right way. It was the safest and best way it could have been handled for me being overly eager to get this boy home with no other training first. Java did have a mild blood nose after this but nothing else. It was me who put both him and Ben in this position. No damage was done and we got him home safe. He never put his head over the wrong side of the bar again. Thank you, Ben, again.

Java

10

Breeding

It was the year 2000. The planet didn't blow up and all the computers in the corporate world coped with changing from 1999 to 2000. If you are of a similar age to me, you will understand the theories and fears of this time in our history as humans raced to fix previous programming limitations.

The property was going well. We had built double fencing for Java's paddock, as he had grown up out of a herd and was unsocialised. It broke my heart but he was used to it, and we always had other horses over the next paddocks.

We tried to put him with one of the mares we had. Hazel was a lovely quarter horse-cross mare we had got for Tom. She was a gem. Anyone could ride her, and she would look after them. I confirmed she was in season and we let them go in the round yard we had built. Horses do this naturally all the time, right? What could possibly go wrong?

We let Hazel and Java both loose at the same time and watched. Java had no manners and was so keen that he just barged, and jumped all over the place. Hazel, being a lady, kicked and screamed and ran as fast as she could. Java was more athletic and faster, so it was of no use, and it didn't help that we had them in a confined 20-metre diameter round yard.

When Hazel couldn't get away anymore, she squealed and kept kicking. Java kept trying, even with me running, yelling and trying to separate them. After a couple more minutes, Hazel's kicks finally had an impact and Java's erect penis copped a hoof. Java suddenly stood quietly, and now we could catch them both. Me and my free-loving ideas may have cost us our stallion.

By the time the vet arrived, Java had three hematomas forming on his body. The two on his chest were the worst. One was already as big as a tennis ball. But the vet wasn't worried about them when Java's manhood was at stake.

Apparently, stallions quite commonly have their penises broken. Fun fact, not.

Java was given a sedative that was designed to relax his manhood, which had already very quickly retracted after the kick. There was a bit of blood coming out but once the sedative truly kicked in, the vet was able to do a thorough examination and we were lucky there was no permanent damage. In future, I would go to 'plan B' for serving. I called Gail and asked if Matilda's mum was still a viable broodmare, which she was. My next question was if Java's father could serve her, and I would take her pregnant. Gail cared so much about her horses, so her answer was a polite but firm 'no'.

The stallion's arthritis was too bad now and it was painful for him to serve, but she encouraged me to still take the mare, as she was a dream to serve and foal. It would be good for both Java and me – we needed a collective confidence to get this breeding thing going and an easy experience to begin with would help.

Josie was a sweetheart of a French thoroughbred, 14.1hh.

She was a registered ASH from when they opened the books up and she was also the mother of Matilda. Within a few weeks of owning her, we put her to Java. Plan B for serving was so much easier, safer and had no vet bills. This method was far more appropriate for where these horses were at. We teased Josie over the teasing board fence to Java and she was spot on. I haltered Java while Tom brought Josie into the paddock. Java reared with joy, but I was now used to handling him and settled him before leading him to within ten metres of Josie. Then I let Java go. He ran straight at Josie, who was a very experienced mare and simply stood like a rock.

Hazel must have had a good impact with Java and his manners as he stopped and just sniffed and assessed things better this time. It's very clever and interesting to watch. He stood at the side and sniffed and pushed the mare on her back and wither with his muzzle, checking she was not going to react. Josie was perfect and just stood, relaxed, and encouraging. Now that was a lot more pleasant for everyone concerned. After a successful serve, Java then dropped his head on her neck and almost went to sleep. *That sounds familiar.* This is when I would clip the lead back on and separate them. Safe and successful, got to love that.

On 31 December 2001, just before midnight, Swassis, meaning 'our little girl' in Navajo, I think, was born. A beautiful chestnut filly. I was smitten. She was perfect. We didn't imprint foals as per the vague definition, but I did do my version to make handling easier. Horses giving birth and foals statistically need to show certain behaviours, or steps need to be taken within certain time frames. A bit like the agar test sheet for human babies. These steps need to occur in a certain order and within an average time frame to give everyone confidence no issues with either the foaling process or the foal itself have occurred.

I had great information from my university study and like all expectant grandparents, had my laminated sheets of information, and timed each process to ensure all were within normal range. *Starting to see a pattern of being very prepared and more hypervigilant than your average person with it. Note to self, is this a good thing that I am becoming hypervigilant? Again, if I could talk to my younger self I'd say, 'In the right circumstances, this is a brilliant thing. Don't let anyone use it against you. It is a skill that not everyone has; you just need to try to balance your thoughts.'*

However, having friends over that night and me running in and out constantly trying to sneak a peak of the birth did make watching *Bridget Jones's Diary* very slow. Our friends convinced me to not go out for a little while. That was when Swassis was born. Once the foal and mare bond, the foal will usually stand within an hour to ninety minutes, have their first nurse then lie down and have a sleep.

The second time, they get up and have a second feed – that is when the mare will then teach them life skills to ensure they listen, follow, and can get away from a predator as quickly as possible. The mare will teach the foal to walk, trot, canter, turn, back, and move laterally – all within a few minutes. This is one of the most fascinating processes and life skill lessons I think you can ever watch as a horse trainer.

Then they have another sleep, which is a big one. That's when I then start to handle the foal. When Swassis got up from this sleep I put my arms around her rump and shoulders to cradle her. Naturally, she bubbled a bit to try to get away, just like nature programmed her. It didn't take much to just cradle her gently and when she relaxed, soften my arms. I then taught her to lead with me cradling. I would do this ten times or more a day so that within a few days it was a non-issue. Then, I would pick up her feet, touch her all over and practice putting my finger in her mouth for future worming and medicating, etc.

We would play in the paddock, and she was starting to run up to see me whenever I went in. Swassis had now got to the point of trusting me so much and enjoying my company that I was starting to be played with like another foal, but she was gentle with me. It was when she started rearing up and landing her front legs gently on my shoulders for a full-on cuddle that I decided we needed some more boundaries. I figured this wasn't going to be as much fun when she was 500 kilos. It was my firstborn.

Josie and Swassis at one day old

This is probably the time that liberty work with horses started accelerating even more with me. The difference between a horse wanting to be with you on their terms and them respecting and seeing you as a leader to staying with you, even though there were other things or horses to go to. Having to put boundaries in place that you feel you are going backwards, and the horse is questioning whether you are just another predator. There is an ultimate fine line between being fair, and not asking too much. That is an art.

Swassis in training

11

Life changes

My job was full-on. I was managing 130 people, had a massive budget and was reporting to high levels of management. I had been working crazy hours for eight years now. I was in a good position to excel further if I wanted with my career in the corporate world, but my heart was always wanting to make horses full-time. I had experienced some health issues the previous year and was told the chances of me having children were very low. If I wanted them, I needed to start thinking about things. I was 32 years old when told this and was starting to regret that I held this off. I then became a health nut and pretty much my body was my temple for the year. I was super fit and lean and thought if I couldn't have children it wasn't meant to be. We decided to just see what happened. I wasn't interested at that stage in looking into anything further if kids didn't happen.

The following year, I was pregnant. I was, as to be expected, over-the-top with being careful of everything I ate. I barely drank alcohol previously but stopped everything, including coffee. I still rode throughout my entire pregnancy, until eight months. I was blessed to only be very unwell for the first 12 weeks, then an easy run the rest of the pregnancy, although I did put on 20 kilos.

When I was seven months pregnant, we had another foal due. We had bred Tea to Java the previous year and she was now due. The night she foaled was horrible, weather-wise. The rain was pelting in, and it was quite cold for spring. In between blustering rain showers, I would go in and out to check on her. Mares have this ability, if they are in the first stage of labour, to delay the birth if interfered with too much and can delay the birth for more than a day.

I was always very careful to have low lighting consistently over the foaling paddock so I could nick in and out to have a peak without the mare noticing. We missed the birth but when I saw the foal it was completely out with the mare standing. The foal had both back legs through the gate and was slipping in the mud trying to get up. We dragged the foal away from the gate and noticed the filly was still struggling to get up. We had the timer going and the filly was now outside of the normal criteria for a healthy foal to stand. I was getting worried. I had thought, initially, this was due to the foal getting stuck in the gate and slipping in the mud. The birth must have been incredibly quick, and this filly was big. She eventually managed to stand but this was quite slow compared to the time she should have taken.

Tea now sniffed her foal, but instead of acting motherly and enticing the foal to drink, Tea was non-committal.

The foal was acting slow, at best. It was like her normal instinct to try to suckle off her mum didn't exist. After a short time, Tea calmly walked away from her foal. That's when I called the vet. He took his time coming and said that this was quite common for maiden mares. From all the information I had learnt at university and all the stories I had heard from the foaling downs there, and my own, I knew this wasn't right. I tried to explain to the vet the foal was acting like it was brain-damaged but he just shrugged me off.

We held the mare and tried to get the foal to attach, but even with the small amounts of milk she got it was not a good attachment. We had to move Tea and her foal into one of our stables to try to confine the foal and give her some treatment. Both Ruth and her husband came over to help, so we had four sets of arms trying to control the mare and foal in the stable so the vet could try to treat and medicate the foal to give it a chance. As I hadn't had any time to work with the foal, mother nature kicked in. The foal would leap around trying to get away, causing itself further distress.

The vet was trying to get an IV-line in. The foal jumped around so much blood started spraying against the walls of the stable. It was hard for me to hold the foal due to my belly. I then got thrown against a stable wall. This is when my sister, Ruth, put her foot down and said, 'Get out, you shouldn't be in here.' The vet turned and looked at me and asked why. Ruth said, 'She is seven months pregnant.' The vet was also now yelling at me to get out. *I know stupid, I shouldn't have been in there and was lucky to get away with it.* I remember then watching from outside the stable crying and feeling helpless. I created this situation and couldn't help. I can't remember exactly what the vet gave the foal but after treatment, he left and said to try to help the foal feed and it should all work out.

The foal was managing to have some feeds but the tell-tale signs of milk all over her face were saying attachment was not good. As the day progressed, things got worse. This foal was not running or acting the way other newborns did. She then started walking into fences. We had low troughs and she then started walking into them and fell in. We got her out and she just continued to walk around in a daze. I rang the vet again and at this stage, we put the mare and foal in a double stable.

All we could do was stand at each end and when the foal came near the wall, turn it before it hit the wall. When I called the vet and explained it was now like she was blind, he got very angry and advised me he had done nothing to cause this. Once he listened to me, I explained I was not accusing, I was telling him the current symptoms. The vet arrived close to an hour later, very apologetic and with his tail between his legs. He explained he had misdiagnosed, and the foal was what was called a 'dummy' foal or a 'maladjusted' foal. The theory back then was, for whatever reason, the foal was born too quickly and had suffered oxygen deprivation and hence brain damage. The mare had not run milk before birthing and everything had looked great. The foal was 36 hours old now and things were not good. The process back then for dealing with this was for both mare and foal to get hospitalised. The foal would then be placed in a semi-coma state. The mare would get constantly milked and the foal stomach fed for over a week. They would then attempt to bring the foal out of this state. At the time, the success rate was about 50 per cent that the foal would then survive and thrive like a normal birth. We decided to give this a go.

Tea was a great horse and Ruth and I had done lots of work with her, so she was great to handle and float load. I tried to put her on the float, and she refused. This continued for about ten minutes and time was of the essence. Tea was never like this.

We put the foal in the float by literally carrying it and one of us held her down, by sitting gently on her neck, then continued to try to get Tea in. This caused Tea to get even more anxious. She didn't want us going anywhere. We then decided to take just the foal and milk Tea. The worst-case scenario was, that if I couldn't get Tea to the hospital, I would just continue to milk her. That is when everything changed. While the vet was milking Tea, the foal began to seize. If you haven't seen an animal or human seizure before, it is very unpleasant. We already had a lot of hay on the floor of the float and so the foal was semi-protected. This was incredibly distressing for everyone involved. Once the foal stopped having the seizure, the vet gave her some sedation, stating, 'This will stop her having another,' so we could continue with our plan.

Five minutes later, she started again. This seizure was about the same in the length of time but now the foal was exhausted and with sedation on board very easy to handle. While the foal was still lying on the floor of the float the vet gave her a second lot of sedation. He was confident this was our best option to continue with our current plan. The vet was almost finished milking the mare when I heard the now-familiar sound of a third seizure. Tom was with the foal, so I looked at the vet's eyes and I knew our plans were about to change. I asked the vet whether our plans were still viable. If further sedation was an option, he replied, 'sadly not.' Any more sedation and the foal wouldn't make it anyway. We brought Tea to her baby and let her sniff her and watch as the vet gave the foal a final dose of sedation and put her to sleep permanently to stop her pain.

The devastation we felt was just crushing. I was now worried if I was going to risk my own pregnancy by being so sad. I was assured my baby would be fine. Although this vet misdiagnosed, I did not blame him. I learnt early you cannot play the what-if game, you just need to take it as a lesson and educate your mind if anything could have been done better. The best thing this vet did advise is how to treat the mare for her to grieve and cope in the best way. This I will never forget, and I have used this with all our animals since it does help in my view. The vet advised us to not take the foal away from her mum. He said to just leave them together in the stable. The mare will continue to watch over her until she has realised there is no point. He said this normally takes anywhere from 36 to 48 hours. We left them together as instructed and fed Tea, watching as she carefully walked around her foal constantly checking it with her muzzle and ensuring no wood shavings from the stable floor were on her. Tea was very calm and continued to dote over her foal for the next 40 hours. Then, sure enough, as the vet had predicted, she started not caring whether the foal was getting covered in wood shavings anymore and she started looking out the stable wanting to leave.

We walked Tea out and she was calm although depressed, but not frantic or even looking for her foal. We placed her in her paddock where we had dug a hole for her baby so she could watch. Tea was eating grass near the hole when we wheeled her baby into the paddock in a wheelbarrow. She didn't come any closer until we dropped her baby in the hole. With that, she just let out a soft nicker and gently walked over. We just stood with her while she looked down on her baby, still, cold, and lifeless. I cuddled Tea and cried into her mane until I couldn't anymore.

Tea then gently walked a short distance away and began to eat. Her eyes would glance across at us as we covered her foal in soil, but she never lifted her head again until it was completed. Whoever says horses don't understand has no idea. Our devastation of Tea losing her foal took a long time to soften and as I type now, I am still brought to tears. We named Tea's foal T2 and placed a plaque on the outside rail of our round yard, not far from her resting place. Four or five years later, when I was doing more research, I came across an article on linking human births where the baby had not gone through the birthing canal for a long enough time having possible effects on them. They referenced a recent discovery by a man called Madigan, and what he had done with horses. Excuse my bastardisation of explaining this, but the thought process was that, in horses, if the birth had been too quick, and the foal was not squeezed enough in the birthing canal, a hormone wasn't released. This, in turn, doesn't signal to the brain the foal is out of the womb and the foal needs to breathe and do all the other things a newborn foal has to do.

I then watched a video of a 'dummy' foal, which was identical to how T2 was. They then simply put a pressure rope around the foal's chest and dragged the foal for a little while. Then they took the rope off. Within a few minutes, the foal shook its head and neck and then acted like someone had hit the reset button and got up and acted normal. Attached to the mare, ran, played. I watched the video again and again and just cried. There was nothing I could do; I couldn't go back in time.

Post-losing T2, I decided to leave full-time employment in the corporate world and be a full-time mum. I was blessed my husband supported this and I was really looking forward to this chapter of my life.

All the literature you read cannot prepare you for what can happen or really explain what and how your hormones make you feel. Due to having a relatively small pelvis, my baby hadn't dropped like expected. I was offered a c-section or an induction labour. I chose the induction.

I always say to other women now who are pregnant, 'Just remember, it's not the process, focus on the outcome.' The hospital did the induction and sent me home telling me to have a sleeping pill, so I got some rest. Me being me, I didn't have the sleeping pill, as I didn't want to take anything in case it affected the baby, even though I was told it wouldn't. I thought I was strong enough to deal with everything. In short, when the induction kicked in, I was straight away put into contractions every three minutes, and they just got more painful as time passed. It took 12 hours of labour before my baby even dropped into the right position.

I can remember clock-watching and mathematically calculating everything in my head, trying to work out how much longer and when the pain would stop. Things got more painful and so I asked for the least damaging drug, which was gas. I think the only reason it helped was it made me focus.

Things got worse and so I was given Pethidine. What a mistake that was. It was horrible. It just knocked me out in between contractions, to then wake into a world of pain constantly. Things were very slow to progress. My body just never kicked in to push like normal labours.

When it was time to birth, my body was spent. They tried a vacuum, but it failed. Forceps, it failed. A team came running in and said an emergency c-section was needed.

Just as I was about to get wheeled out, another obstetrician assessed me and advised the baby was stuck too low and a c-section was not an option. Past this, even though I had no more pain relief and my eyes were open I don't have much more memory of it all. I remember looking at the ceiling and thinking I don't care anymore if I die if the baby is ok. I was put up in stirrups and my pelvis was dislocated by two nurses both pushing my knees down. Then cut in a couple of places. Forceps were then successful in pulling out our baby boy 20 hours after contractions had begun. He was blue and needed oxygen, so he was rushed off.

I made his father promise previously that if something happened to me during the process don't let him out of your sight. His father stayed with him while they fixed me. The obstetrician then told me how lucky we both were and that others in a similar situation don't always have such a great outcome.

My baby came back looking a better colour, already had bruising on his face and his head was a bit squished on one side. To me, he was the best-looking baby I had ever seen. (S*ee what I mean about hormones?)*

Liam became the centre of my life, as all first babies do. I could write another novel without blinking about the joy children brought to my life. The intense feelings of love and responsibility are overwhelming. My ethnic side came out with ensuring a warm olive oil massage nightly for the first year of Liam's life was essential. From six weeks of age, we would read a story to him every night until he could read himself. I used flashcards from six weeks old as a game. I researched diets and best current practices. I homemade all the food and gave the best of everything I could. Tom continued to work long hours and travel was becoming more and more common. I was running the property and horses we had, as well as bringing up my son. It was hard – and very lonely at times – but I loved my life.

We had a trip to the USA and Canada, focusing on some horse places I specifically wanted to visit. Montana, Colorado and Wyoming – all incredible locations. My favourite place was Silver Gate in Montana. It was a small town outside of Yellowstone National Park where you could only get to half of the year, through the Beartooth Highway. Magical!

I was lucky enough to go on a few horse rides there and it broadened my mind on some management theories. Horses are horses. That was a great confidence booster for me. As naïve as I was for some reason, I thought horses overseas would be different - not the case. They speak the same language regardless.

I was now looking at getting another broodmare to build our breeding stock. It took some time but I eventually found a four-year-old, 15hh, black mare that was a registered ASH. She was in New South Wales and was owned by a vet. She was handled but not broken in due to an accident she incurred when she was a yearling.

The owner told me she had spooked in a thunderstorm and gone through a fence. She had severed halfway through her deep digital flexor tendon in a leg and so he thought she would never hold up to being a riding horse but be a perfect broodmare. I bought her sight unseen as I felt this vet should know what he was talking about, and he had spent a lot of time chatting with me on the phone. A bit like the first conversation with Gail, I felt I had just gone through an interview. I discussed what our plans were and how we wanted to breed quality ASH that had the optimal physical and mental start to produce brilliant riding horses. The owner was excited for me and arranged to have the mare trucked to an ASH stud only a few hours from me, as he had other clients' horses going on that trip.

A week later, we met Koko at a Stud a few hours away from us. She was stunning. Ruth came with me to pick her up and we both felt this mare was going to produce my perfect horses. She floated home with no incidents, and I was patting myself on the back for being patient and working so hard to build my dream.

Before putting Koko to Java, I wanted to get her handling better. One thing that stood out that I had come across a few times was when I went to drench (worm) her, she would get very upset and anxious. Her head would go up and she would run backwards like I was hurting her. I initially put it down to previous bad experiences on her behalf, however, it never really improved that much, regardless of how much time I put in.

Although I had no intention of starting Koko to be ridden, I mouthed her with a bridle, hoping this would help the situation. It helped a little, but the issue was always simmering away. I had experienced this with other peoples' horses before and often thought, 'dental, neck, back or possibly behavioural.' But I still felt there was so much I didn't know and was over-analysing things. Or so people kept telling me.

12

Railroad switch

I continued working around our property and my dream of breeding and bringing up the perfect horses. I was offering agistment and had created a business on the side. I was pregnant again and, at the ripe old age of 36, I kept getting told it was a geriatric pregnancy. Everything was going well, technically ... besides my weight. This time, I was still experiencing nausea through to seven months in and the only thing that helped was to eat. By the end of the pregnancy, I had put on 30 kilos – and I was only 60 kilos at the start. I felt – and had been told – that first births are completely different to any subsequent births that follow, and I was hoping that would be the case.

About a month or so before the baby was due, I was told it was in a breach position. Again, I was offered a c-section. Other options were having a manual manipulation to turn the baby but, more than likely, the stress would prompt the intervention of a c-section, anyway. The only hospital offering to wait and see what happened advised that, if I went into labour and the baby was still in breach, if it was big and got stuck like my first pregnancy, it was quite possible that we would both die. Not what you want to hear! My first son was just shy of nine pounds and I was advised this baby would be of similar size.

I was blessed that this hospital had a birthing centre, and we went and discussed with them any other options before I agreed to anything.

One of the midwives came out with a ratty photocopied piece of paper with a dodgy diagram of a woman in a dog-like position and instructions on how to do self-acupuncture. I had never had acupuncture done on myself, only horses. And I'd never been behind the needles. The information sheet also wrote about getting moxibustion candles. But, I thought, what have I got to lose? I brought the candles home, watched them burn while wedged between my toes, and then went into my weird position for the instructed amount of time. I did this, as that piece of paper directed, over two days.

I was walking around with Liam, doing the horse feeds, when it hit. I felt this massive movement of the baby and grabbed onto a gate and started yelling. It was summer and I only had a thin cotton top on. I saw my stomach move this way and that and remember thinking that I looked like one of the actors in the movie *Alien*. This was incredibly painful – but it wasn't labour. It only lasted a couple of minutes and then stopped. I rang my doctor and told him that something had happened and that I'd better come in. He saw me straight away, as I'd already had a fright just a few weeks earlier when I had fainted due to heat exhaustion trying to still do everything I normally did in my non-pregnant life – in 40-degree heat! I'd been warned then that I could trigger an early birth if I didn't get help on the hotter days, which I was now doing.

So, I arrived at the doctor, wondering what the issue was this time and it only took him a minute to feel before he announced, 'Well, whatever you did, the baby is now turned the right way and ready to go.'

I found an amazing midwife, who was also an acupuncturist. She was brilliant. I saw her a couple of times a week and every time I waddled out from seeing her, I felt my baby was going to fall out.

My second birth was completely different. My body knew what to do and, although I was being induced, the birth was considered 'normal' in medical terms.

I only had a shot of something to help calm me and stop me from crawling around the floor, vomiting. Twelve hours from the time my labour had officially started, we were the proud parents of a second boy, Ethan.

The intense feeling of love and devotion was just as powerful as before. I love these hormones. Ethan was one of these special babies, the midwife explained to me. After he was born, he shuffled his way across my body to attach himself and feed. I never even knew human babies were capable of this. It's a short-lived skill, though, and they lose the ability shortly after birth and don't regain it until later in their development.

Both my boys are the best achievement in my life. Both so incredible and such different personalities.

On the same day I had Ethan, our beautiful dog, Mallik, passed away a few hours later. He was almost 13 years old and, for such a large breed, that was exceptional. He was an amazing dog, and my heart was so confused with the ecstatic happiness of first having my son and then losing one of my best friends within hours. We had Mallik frozen, so when I came home from the hospital, I could cuddle him before burying him. I will never forget the look on the gentleman's face that was sitting in the excavator while watching me cuddle a 70-kilo, frozen, fuzzy dog. He must have thought I had gone nuts after my last son was born. But without writing another book, I honestly couldn't explain the level of devotion and love I had for this Alaskan Malamute. He had been my confidant, protector and friend.

A few days after Ethan was born, Koko had her first foal, Chika. The name means 'our son' in one of the Native American languages. He was a stunning liver chestnut colt. I felt so blessed, although I was still sad about losing Mallik. I had two amazing children I thought I would never be able to have. I had our dream property and my dreams of building a horse business and promoting best practices by breeding our horses were all coming into line.

Two weeks after having Ethan, I started Swassis. She was now a five-year-old and I felt I had to get her going. Swassis was a very easy horse to start. True to my beliefs of putting all the right foundations and groundwork in, the next level of riding was just a breeze. Just as well, too, as everyone knows how busy you get with two young kids and a husband busy working. We had also bred Tea again – and this time everything went perfectly. We now used foaling alarms on our mares, which made things a lot easier, and it meant we were more likely to be there for the birth. The night Tea foaled this time was at a time when I was alone with the boys. I was still breastfeeding my youngest son through the night and, luckily, my oldest boy always slept well through the night. It was three am when the alarm went, which woke Ethan up. Of course, that meant he wanted a feed. I rang my wonderful neighbour who was forever there for me in times of crisis, and she showed up with torch in hand while I sat in the middle of the paddock on a deck chair – feeding my son while watching our newest foal find her way to her feet. She was quick. Quick to stand, quick to feed and light on her feet. We never looked over her completely with the torch. We were excited (*and I think I was permanently exhausted!*) and we assumed she must be perfect.

But the next morning, in the light, I noticed one of her front legs wasn't right. From her fetlock down, it was bent and barely straightened to touch the ground. She was still up and about and running like a happy, healthy foal. I got the vet up that day, and he explained her leg must have just been bent while the mare was pregnant. A little injection to relax the tendon and a customised gutter bracket gaffer taped to her hoof was his recommendation and, two days later, it had clearly worked. Leg perfect! She was stunning. Three weeks younger than Chika, this was Shilo. I named her Shilo as it translates to 'quick'.

I loved having my boys and filling my days with them. I started getting help for one day a week from one of their grandparents, so I could try to build my business of giving lessons about horses, as well as have time to do some maintenance around the property. We also got a farm hand for half a day a week to help keep on top of things. Tom was away a lot, either overseas or interstate. There was a lot of time when both boys and I were by ourselves. My boys, property and horses were my life.

It was around this time that I lost my beloved Starbuck. He presented with colic-like symptoms but, being 30 years old, I explained to the vet attending that there would not be any surgery or going to the hospital. Our property – and me – were his home and happy place.

We set up a drip and I managed the nursing with the help of Ruth and Christine if he didn't come good with the normal medications. The vet then did a peritoneal tap and collected some fluid from his belly to identify the severity of the colic. I knew as soon as I saw the vet draw a second syringe to double-check the results. The liquid should have been clear to pale yellow. It was bright red. This meant it was too late and things were already twisted or ruptured. We euthanised him on the spot. Starbuck had been in our lives for 27 years. He had spent more time with me than any human. He had been my saviour on so many levels. This hit me hard.

***

One day, just after Ethan's first birthday, I was changing him on the change table when he went stiff and started shaking. I knew immediately he was seizing but didn't know what to do. I picked him up and ran into the lounge room and put him on a play blanket on the floor, then opened the door to outside where several people were building a new horse structure. I screamed at the top of my voice and my cries made Tom, my brother-in-law, and our farm hand all run in. When they got inside, Ethan stopped shaking and was still and starting to turn blue. I began screaming and crying. Tom was on the phone to emergency services, who were trying to calm everything down. My brother-in-law had worked in a hospital previously and picked Ethan up with a gentle squeeze on his chest, which was enough to start him breathing again. That split second when I thought Ethan had stopped breathing, my whole world had collapsed. The fear was overpowering. When the ambulance arrived and checked Ethan out, they advised it was a febrile seizure, which was quite common. They advised that he probably hadn't stopped breathing, but that his breaths would have been very shallow in his little body.

This had purely been caused by the speed of the temperature in his body rising too quickly and he developed tonsilitis shortly after. All medical checks were done and, because I was now feeling scared, I started attending First Aid courses. Over the next 18 months, Ethan had five seizures all up. Some when he would shake, some catatonic where he would just freeze. He always put himself in my arms every time before he had one. We went to several specialists and were advised even though his situation was very unusual with the length of time and types of seizures he had, he would still probably grow out of them. Monitoring Ethan and any presentation of future illnesses that cause the temperature to rise became a little obsessive for me. Looking back, I can understand why.

Over this time, we had also bred Koko again to Java. She had another beautiful liver chestnut colt. This one was a thicker set and a lot richer in colour. His temperament was different from his brother's. He was more reactive to things. This was Giha, meaning 'other son'. For everyone out there googling these names to check their authenticity, I can no longer find the language sheets I used. All the names we used were from several different dialects. Chika was now a two-year-old and I needed to put some more work into him. It was a windy day, and he was spooked but it was the only time I had, thanks to having a grandparent over to help with the boys.

I was doing a very common groundwork exercise with a fence next to me. Changing reins back and forth between me and the fence until he started relaxing. The wind was howling, and it was about to start raining again. I had just got Chika to the point where he had licked and chewed, thought about things, and was coming down with his head dropping when I heard a crack. I don't know how long I was on the ground. I had blacked out. When I woke, I looked up to see Chika standing above me with his head relaxed and just staring at me. My face hurt. I felt my face and touched my nose, which was swollen. I had blood all over me. A lot of blood. I stood up and was lightheaded. There was a massive branch on the ground behind Chika. It must have snapped off and that was the noise I heard. Chika must have tried to bolt away and went through me. He didn't have anywhere else to go – the branch was right behind him. I went to the hospital, where I was told my nose was broken and, due to blacking out, I needed to be monitored overnight, as a minimum. After waiting for six hours and still not seeing a doctor, I went home. There was no one there to do the horse feeds and my boys were getting scared. Tom's mum stayed in a bungalow we had built on the property that night. I survived the night and now just have a lumpy nose, and so did

Chika. You know it must have been a hard hit when your horse has bone calcification from the hit as well.

***

The demands of the property and horses could be stressful, and a few months later we went away on what was supposed to be a holiday. I then got a call from my neighbour that when she went to do the horse feeds, she had found Giha in another paddock next to his mum, Koko. He was only six weeks old. Giha was bleeding a lot from his head and had several lacerations from the wire fencing. One just in front of one ear and another cut behind the opposite ear. Half his face was paralysed. I decided it wasn't fair to stay away from the property and have the neighbour deal with our issues and we arrived home the next

Koko and Giha

day. This was incredibly stressful. To be honest, it was such a difficult time that I cannot even remember where we had gone on holiday. Giha had 35 stitches to his head, which had taken the vet five hours. Nobody could work out what happened and why he must have run into the fence. He couldn't drink properly and wouldn't be caught again by strangers to have his medications. But after a few hours, I was catching him easily and managing his medications. He was getting feelings back in his face a few days later and some movement back. The one thing that stood out again was his similarity to Koko now with his reaction when his head went up in the air. No one else was noticing this trait and understandably concentrating on the immediate medical issues.

***

Life seemed to be flying by with how busy the boys kept me, the property, and breeding. My boys were aged five and two years old when their father asked for a separation. The one sentence that stuck in my mind was, 'You mean nothing to me.' I asked him to leave that day. I will not mention anything else to do with this out of respect for everyone. My life had just been derailed. In a blink, I was a single mother with two young boys to bring up – and I needed to think fast.

13

My new journey

Life can change in a heartbeat. No matter what you have pictured in your mind, what you think the way your life will play out like, that vision can be changed in an instant. I started seeing a psychologist to help me cope and to assist me in getting my life and future sorted. I cannot recommend this enough. To have an objective person listen to you in a way that is safe and non-judgemental can be a saving grace. Well, it was for me. To have someone say that you are worth a lot and that you do mean a lot to many people. The hurt and emotional damage some people can cause with throwaway comments when you're in a world of pain can be overwhelming and it does help to have a confidant you can talk to. Divorce and shared custody of children is extremely difficult for everyone and was the hardest time of my life. No one knows the full truth but yourself, and the reality is that no one else is really interested.

Tea had a third foal that I named Kuri. He was a stunning bay colt. He was sold as a yearling to a promising young rider. They visited me six months later to explain to me how they lost him due to an infected petal bone. The poor girl and family – how devastating! I never bred Tea again after that.

Tea and Kuri

I did breed Koko for a third time and the foal was due the following year. I was now focused on ramping up my business more with my lessons, agistment and retraining of horses. When I had my sons, they were my priority, no matter what. When I didn't have them, on the days they were with their dad, work was my focus and I was determined to do everything I could to continue my dream. I had the option to go back to the corporate world, where I would earn great money but looking after my kids would be made difficult. I didn't want to put them in care, as I now felt I was missing out on part of their lives anyway. I chose to build my business and work when I could so that I could spend as much time with my boys as possible. This meant funds would be tight, but I had as much time as I could with my boys. Time with them outweighed anything else.

***

I was scared but excited. All my choices of what I could do with horses and the path to follow were finally mine. The limitations, of course, were linked to the responsibilities that came with being a mum, as well as working and managing the property. I still had my idealism of changing the world with horses for the better. I continued to educate myself by attending clinics and subscribing to veterinary websites to ensure I was giving the best care and training I could.

It was 2008; I was 39 and single with two kids, a property and a business to manage. I was busy. I wasn't interested in finding a companion/partner/boyfriend or whatever you want to call it. I just wanted to be me. I wanted to be kind to myself and build my confidence back. I was confident with horses, but I lacked a lot of self-esteem and struggled with the niggling feeling that there must be something wrong with me. The weight of always being abandoned played heavily in my mind. What was so wrong with me that no one loved me enough to stay and allow me to be me? *Again, if I could speak to myself at that time now, I would say, 'There is nothing wrong with you, girl. You are an amazing, caring mother and person. A hard worker and honest. Don't worry about what other people think.'*

We are so hard on ourselves to be perfect. I was still best friends with Christine. She has been and always will be my sounding board and great support. One dear lifetime friend that always steps up! What a blessing! Monique and Janine were also still in my life, we just didn't spend a lot of time together, as everyone's life gets so busy.

I was starting to learn new skills around the property and had to take on more roles I hadn't done previously. Fencing, chainsawing, fixing things, you name it. I no longer had the farm hand, as I couldn't afford to pay anyone but also didn't trust many men. I'd always thought, even on a 'good' day, that I was plain to look at, but since becoming single I was starting to get a lot of (unwanted) attention. Now I was confused. I had little voices in my head, thinking I would be single for the rest of my life because no one would be interested. I know I can be a handful as I think outside the box; I am passionate and ethical to the point of annoying, but I never wanted to feel again that there was something wrong with me. I needed to feel some genuine self-worth again. Any interest in a man needed to stay on the back burner. I needed to heal my soul.

I will never forget once the financial settlement had occurred how I was treated by some people. I had the property and I had to work to make sure I kept it. I think a lot of people thought I was on an easy street. Properties are not cheap or easy to run. If I kept the property, I thought I would keep my sanity, and still be able to work my hours so I could still do everything for the boys and continue to follow my dreams of educating people with horses. I wanted to be the best person I thought I could be, so I was the best example to my boys and living the happiest life I could so that I could be a good mother. I was, and still am, a very 'real' type of person. Glamour, the material possessions you have do not make the person you are. A parent's guilt will always make you question every decision you have made. Time is the most precious gift anyone can give you in my mind.

I continued to get a lot of unwanted attention from a few blokes who I didn't care for or want. I didn't trust that they weren't just after what I had, rather than who I was. I just wanted to be me. I will never forget one summer evening before it got dark, and I was by myself riding Swassis in the foaling paddock at liberty. No saddle, no bridle or halter. I would practice riding with just my hands on her neck to build our relationship and work on my balance. It was great fun. I was practising cantering circles, one way, then the next which was going brilliantly. I had a bottle of wine on one fence post and a glass on the other. Swassis had got into the pattern, by my third glass. She simply idled up to the post so I could grab my glass, then move to the next so I could fill it and have a drink. I didn't have my boys that weekend and thought I needed to try to start to enjoy my life a little. Ruth showed up to check on me and see if I was ok. Half a bottle of wine in, I was great. I just advised her I was now going to practice flying lead changes at the canter. Go figure, things didn't quite go to plan, and I slipped right off and fell on the ground at a canter. I wasn't hurt. I just rolled over onto my back and laughed and laughed. I think it was the first time I had a real belly laugh for years.

Riding Swassis at liberty

14

You are worth the world

It was 2009 and just as I was starting to enjoy being me, things were about to change. A neighbour from up the road on a different property telephoned me. Russell. He was calling to ask if I wanted to organise a hay contractor and take the hay from his property, as he knew I was always after extra hay. He lived with his two sons and his daughter lived with their mum. I had heard on the street rumour mill that he had been single for a few years. Russell explained he had broken his arm falling off a motorbike, his oldest son had a broken wrist, and his youngest son was dealing with a broken growth plate in his knee. All accidents from motorbikes. He explained that picking up hay from their property wasn't an option for any of them now. I was thinking, motorbikes don't sound that great. I then explained that I couldn't, as I was now by myself running the property with my boys and had to pick up all my hay, plus hay from another property I had already arranged.

To this comment, Russell said he was sorry to hear I was by myself now. *Apparently, behind closed doors, he was fist-pumping and smiling, I heard later.* We then had an amazing, honest conversation. He had simply asked me how I was managing and told me that he knew how tough it was when your life changed like mine had. I had known Russell as a neighbour before and seen him with his kids, horses and motorbikes – and always thought he seemed like a nice bloke. We had also met a couple of times over the years as neighbours do when passing by, or helping get horses back in paddocks, helping neighbours put out small fires before they get out of hand and the like. I had only ever viewed him as a kind person. Over the next few weeks, we must have talked on the telephone for hours. Unless they have personally experienced it, people don't understand what you go through when you separate or divorce and experience the gut-wrenching feeling of having to share the children who have previously been with you every day of your life as a parent. Russell was so real, so honest and, to this day, the best person I have ever talked to about real soul feelings. He also made me laugh.

Russell asked one day if I could give his youngest son a lift to the bus stop, as he left too early and my oldest was starting school, so it was on my way. Not a problem. We continued to chat on the phone, and I invited him to bring his son over so we could meet. I thought it must be terrifying for a teenage boy to go to some strange woman's house and get in a car with her when he had only seen me a few times in his life. I didn't think anything romantic about it. The day they were coming over, I panicked, thinking, 'Oh my god – what happens if he has the wrong idea?' I couldn't even remember what Russell looked like. I only remembered he was short.

When they showed up, the second I saw Russell and his warm smile my feelings changed instantly. Oh, shit. I initially said I was staying single for at least two years. This man was so great to talk to, though. Relax. I was toilet training Ethan at the time and Ethan decided to show me he could wee without a nappy … in the hallway. Just as well I had floorboards. Russell was so calm and just sat on the couch without running off and being too busy. This shocked me.

We continued to talk on the phone in the days and weeks that followed. I still didn't trust myself to be a good judge of character. I trusted Java and Matilda more than anyone. Both were extremely sensitive and would react like litmus paper to people. I asked Russell to come help me inject all the horses with vaccinations. The truth was that I could do this by myself with my eyes closed – but I wanted to see what they thought of him.

When Russell showed up that day, he seemed a bit agitated. He asked whether I needed him, as my dad and brother-in-law were there helping on the property. I explained they had no experience with horses and would make them nervous. He then changed and relaxed again. I still don't know what that was about, but with my lack of confidence, that was almost a deal breaker. Was there another side to him that I didn't know? Was I willing to take a risk? I reminded myself I had no idea what was going on in his life except what he had told me and to not be so timid. We started vaccinating the easier horses on the property. All Russell had to do was hold the lead rope and calmly pat the horse so they were relaxed for me to insert the needle and inject. All the vaccinations had gone well and we had no issues. I saved Matilda and Java for last. They were the biggest critics. Now Matilda. She hesitated when I gave him her lead to hold her while I prepared to do her vaccination. Her head was raised, and she sniffed the air. Russell then scratched her forehead, and she relaxed under his touch. Her head lowered and she exhaled and was at her calmest. She didn't move while I injected her. That was her approval, now Java. Java could be quite confronting and would raise his head and neck like a giraffe to show his presence to anyone new. He took a fraction longer, but he had the same relaxed reaction to Russell. Java even rubbed back into Russell's hand after I had finished injecting him. Shit, shit, decision made. I thanked Russell for his help and rang

Christine the second he left. I answered her 'hello' by bursting into tears and telling her that Matilda and Java had just given Russell the 'okay'. She laughed as she answered me. 'Poor bloke doesn't know what is coming.'

Russell invited me out for dinner soon after that as a thank you for driving his son. I was tipping it was more than that. It was a lovely night and it definitely felt more like a date. Both of us texting afterwards we should meet up again.

A week or so went by and Russell and I had continued to text and talk over the phone constantly. I had a client at the time whose horse had a leg injury that didn't look great, so I advised them to get a second opinion from a vet. They did so and were advised a course of penicillin. When I asked my client whether she understood the risks of injecting, she told me she did, but three days later I got the call that her horse had suffered a severe procaine reaction. The horse got down on a gravel driveway and thrashed. It survived that but, sadly, when it then needed surgery to clean up its knee, it never woke up from the general anaesthesia. The owner of the horse and her daughter were devastated. I wish the full extent of what can happen when giving these injections would be better explained to horse owners. Until you see the potentially negative consequences yourself, you don't fully understand how serious it can be and maybe you don't take all the precautions. These were amazing people who just lost a six-year-old mare they adored; it was devastating. Russell showed up for a drink, carrying two bottles of red wine. 'Great timing,' I told him. 'My day was not good.'

The client rang shortly after and I noticed Russell listening as I chatted to her. After I got off the phone, he praised me and told me how amazing I was, how giving and thoughtful. It was the best compliment I had heard in a long time. That night, our relationship changed.

Enough of the talk about Russell. *He will be like a peacock strutting around, reading this.*

15

My new life

The longer I was with Russell, the more my confidence grew. We had been together as a couple for about six months now. I felt like I mattered – and it felt like the first time I had truly believed that. Work was getting busier, and I felt we shared the same dreams without limiting each other. Even though we were a couple in every other way, we did not live together. Things can be very complicated with children and blending families can be challenging. We bought another ASH mare. Yella. She was a lovely Palomino stock horse and was 14.3hh and six years old. She had the best personality. We bought her sight unseen, after watching a video and talking to her trainer. She was, supposedly, started under saddle and was too quiet. Alarm bells went off in my mind. I explained to the training centre selling her that she didn't have to be started, as I wanted her for breeding. I could start her myself if I wanted. They insisted she had been ridden under saddle and was fine. She had also had one foal previously, and apparently, everything went smoothly. There was no video of her being ridden and she had leg bandages on in all videos. I asked for photos of her legs without the bandages and, sure enough, one had extreme scarring. People, honestly! Just tell the truth. This was an old wire fence injury and, although it left her with terrible scarring, it was superficial. She wasn't lame in the video. We decided to get her anyway. *I have now learnt that as soon as someone puts music to a video and slows it down, it's probably bullshit and it shows that the person has better skills with a computer than horses.*

When Yella was delivered, the transport truck parked outside the property and led her down the driveway. That was my second alarm bell. Then we saw her. She looked nothing like the photo and was severely dehydrated. The transport man ran down the driveway and back to his truck before I could put two words together. It took us four months to get her back to healthy and ready for the season to breed. I thought I would give her a couple of rides before we put her to Java to breed. I put a saddle on her and did my normal tests when I start a horse or retrain one. Everything was good and she was used to a saddle. I put a bridle on and did some bending on the ground to make sure she understood the bit and yielded to pressure. I also did a few other checks and again she demonstrated she was experienced with a bridle as the video had shown her getting lounged with a bridle on. Everything still looked and felt good. I tend to not get on a horse from the ground, as I think that, no matter how good you are, you twist on their wither. I teach horses to idle up to a ladder or anything high enough that I can step on. No issues so far. When I sat on her, she wasn't too concerned. I asked her to move forward. She had no idea. I knew instantly that no one had ever ridden her.

I treated her then the same as any other starter and just gently encouraged her forward. I rode her for about five minutes and got off. It seemed great for a first ride. I then called the training facility I had bought her from and asked why they lied. I told them I didn't understand that behaviour and reminded them that I had been clear with them and said that it didn't matter if she hadn't been ridden, as I could sort this myself and knew what I was doing. But why lie? If I hadn't been experienced,

I could have got on her and assumed it was all good, which I had been told would be the case. I told them that I might have then given her a harder push – working on the belief that she had been started – and that it would have probably gone pear-shaped. The trainer told me I misunderstood what they had told me. She claimed she had said the horse had been backed, and had a saddle on, but not ridden. I called bullshit. I then proceeded to tell them to start telling people the truth, so people or horses don't get hurt. Honestly, I don't get people a lot of the time.

***

Koko was due with her third foal, and I had the foaling alarm set up in the kitchen. With Russell and his kids coming over for tea for his daughter's birthday and Koko so close to becoming a mum again, I wanted to make sure I juggled everything.

I'd made a beautiful chocolate cake with chocolate icing to look like mud and had put frogs – the lolly type – all over the cake. I was rather pleased with myself. I thought I could do this whole property, kids, blend, work, run my own business thing. Then as we were singing Happy Birthday, I looked at the monitor and realised it was turned off. Maybe I can't do everything, after all! As soon as I turned it on, it was blaring. We all sprinted outside to see Koko and her new foal lying down together. The cord was still attached and the foal's back hooves had just come out. Talk about a birthday with a bang. We all stayed and watched until it was too cold for the kids. That was our third chestnut colt from Koko and Java, two black horses. We named this colt Takota, which, I was told, means friend to everyone. I thought it was appropriate that he showed up during a birthday celebration. This was going to be Russell's riding horse, we decided.

***

I still struggled a lot with sharing the kids, as any parent who has gone through separation or divorce would understand. It is not a normal feeling to not have your children with you all the time. It's like a piece of your heart is missing. I tried to be the best mum I could when they were with me and then put my energy into working on building the business and earning money when I was without them. The first Christmas holidays I had to share them was terrifying to me. To get my mind off it, I suggested to Russell that we could go away. Just get in the car and drive. So, we did. We headed towards the Victorian high country, as I had heard there were a lot of herds of wild brumbies. I had started a few horses by now and had been told brumbies were very hard to catch but, once caught, very easy to start. My understanding was that it's because no one else has messed with these horses, so they have no prior mixed messages or issues and are more of a blank canvas. I wanted to meet someone who could help me experience this.

We had driven for five hours or so and were just following our nose. I had heard the Blue Duck Pub in Anglers Rest past Omeo had a lot of history and was very much a landmark. We made that our destination. I loved the country there. It was stunning. We camped the night next to the river just a bit down from the pub and it was just what I needed. The next day, we decided we would drive around a bit and see if we could find what we were looking for.

Not too far from where we camped, we drove for a little bit and went across a cattle grid. The herd of horses we came across was just stunning. All different colours, not too many either large or small, and there was something familiar with most of them. Some looked like they could be brumbies and others not. We got out and walked among them. Some were friendly, others didn't want a bar of us. They had smaller herds within the valley, and some just ran for the hills when we came into sight and disappeared, while some seemed more relaxed and stayed. We were intrigued. We looked for the closest house we could see and drove in there. It had a sign up, *The Willows*. We got out of the car and started walking to the house when a lady came out and asked if she could help us. We explained we were just having a look around and if the herds of horses were brumbies. She told us that some were. When I asked her who owned them, she told us it was her. This lady was stunning. I am not necessarily talking about her looks. Yes, she was a very good-looking woman, but it was her demeanour of strength, confidence, and friendliness that I was in awe of. She was a bit older than me and presented as a strong woman who had many stories to tell. She introduced herself as Helen.

We asked what her property did, and she told us she bred her own horses, ran horse rides and also offered accommodation. We asked if we could stay for a few days and, as no one else was currently staying with her, we had our pick of either a guest house or one of two rustic cabins away from the house. We picked one of the cabins. It was gorgeous and real. It was like we had just walked back to 150 years ago. It had no power, phone, or utility service, just a gas-bottle fridge, a fireplace and candles. There was also a gas cooktop, a small table with two chairs and two beds. The bathroom was an outside shower made of stone walls and an outside dunny. It was perfect. It was in a small valley within the property and had an overflow from the dam run past the hut and down to a river. We had a different herd of horses on this part of the property.

The property and valley we were in were just magical. It was the first time without my kids that I felt real joy about going away. The next day, we asked to go on a trail ride. A few other people were booked to ride that day too, so we joined up with them in a group for a two-hour ride. I never tell people what I do for a job when going to horse businesses unless I feel like it's appropriate. I would often go to horse trail-riding places and other businesses for my research to see and feel what their horses were like and to see if I could learn anything from their management practices. When asked what level of riding experience I had, I would always simply say, 'basic'. Helen picked out all our horses and matched them pretty much to what we told her our skill level was. We set out through the back of the property and a river. I loved this country. These horses were used to this.

We were single file much of the ride, as this made it easier for Helen to manage the trail safely. We had just ridden up a beautiful open mountain and, when we reached close to the top, we stopped and looked back at the valley and down on Helen's property. Truly beautiful.

One of the other women on the ride was having a little trouble with her horse and was beginning to get nervous. We started off again and entered the bush on a single trail that was not much wider than the horses. The lady having a bit of trouble started asking me what to do, as her horse and her weren't working together. I told her that we should both go up the back and for her to ride in front of me and to try asking and releasing the horse with the reins. I tried to explain how to use her legs and hands as simply and quietly as I could. Helen was up the front and would turn and watch occasionally when the track allowed, to make sure everyone was ok. Russell was riding in front of this lady, so I knew he would block the horse and help if needed. Between us – Russell in front blocking her horse and me behind whispering instructions – her horse started relaxing and so did she. After a few minutes, the lady said, way too loudly, 'Wow this is much better, thank you.'

My new life

Like a hawk, Helen turned and stopped and asked if everything was alright. Again, way too loudly, the lady between Russell and I answered, 'Yep, lots better now after some advice.' Then the question came from Helen, 'So, what do you do for a living?' She was sharp, this one – I couldn't get away with anything. So, I know I have previously said I don't lie … But, well … I do sort of tell white lies sometimes, but only for good and not evil. 'Who, me? I'm a florist.' *This had always been my go-to occupation when I didn't want to tell the truth. It had started when I worked in the corporate world and things were incredibly stressful. We used to always joke and say, I want to be a florist and just play with pretty flowers all day. Later in life, I met a few florists and apparently, it can be very stressful, like all businesses and working with live things and people.*

This little white lie had always helped me to date, but not that day. The lady I had been helping, again, spoke way too loudly. 'Oh really, wow, what a coincidence! So am I.'

You have got to be kidding me! Russell turned his head on his horse to look back at me and smile, as if to say, now you're *bleep*. Then this lady proceeded to ask if I'd been having any trouble getting a flower whose name sounded like the entire alphabet… in Latin. I hesitated for a moment but decided to keep going along with it. 'Yesss …'

This lady then stopped her horse. *Really? Now you can stop your horse and manage it? The difference with a rider when they have a purpose is amazing. When this fellow florist wasn't overthinking she easily stopped her horse. I also learnt never to lie again about being a florist.* This very friendly, loud lady now said at the top of her voice, 'OMG you're lying. You're not a florist. You can't tell us what you are. Oh, let's guess. Do you work for the FBI? You're undercover? The Secret Service? Oh, I get it you're in the sex trade?'

OMG, just stop. By now Helen was bent around looking back at me like I had just murdered someone. So, under my breath, I whispered, 'I'm a horse trainer.'

The lady I am now going to refer to as 'Mouth' – but who was, honestly, lovely – asked me more questions, saying she couldn't hear me. Mouth continued to ask me to repeat until she finally heard, and so did Helen. Mouth then said that made a lot more sense. Russell was sniggering so much he almost fell off his horse, while Helen just simply said, 'Get up here.'

Helen and I then rode together, chatting about horses, training methods, how brilliant some trainers were, how stoic horses are to put up with our bullshit. We talked and talked like there was no one else with us. I had just found a kindred soul, and this was the start of a beautiful friendship. We stayed for almost a week. We went up to the main house to share a meal but tried to stay separate a little at night. Helen drove us all over the property, shared her knowledge of how she ran the place and asked our advice on a range of issues she was facing. She wasn't like a lot of horse people that can be narrow-minded. She was like a sponge. Asking and discussing intricate details of management and training and happily taking the advice we shared with her on board. Helen asked if I would work with a few horses, and she could watch, and we wouldn't have to pay for accommodation. Seemed fair to me. I always find it rewarding when you work with a horse and those watching can appreciate the changes and the importance of trust and the relationship without being bulldozed.

The property had three main areas for herds. There was the land around the accommodation that had all breeding mares with foals at foot and her stallion, Captain, all running together. The paddocks with the riding horses all running in a herd, and the furthest, wildest part of the property for the young herds that were weaned but not trained or started to be trail-riding horses yet. She also had some of the retired or gammy horses in this herd as babysitters to teach the younger ones. Helen had trained all the herds that, if someone drove around tooting the horn of her old Land Rover, they needed to move into the yards. It was great to watch and worked like an alarm clock to know when to go outside and start doing things. She always had extra people working there, mainly from overseas on a working holiday. They would assist with running the property, training horses, taking trails out, gardening, cooking meals, and maintaining the accommodation. Helen welcomed everyone and treated everyone like they had a story worth listening to. She had many friends. Catherine, a neighbour up the road from Helen, was another amazing high-country woman. She ran cattle with her family and would visit Helen often to help with the horses and taking out trails. These women were so strong and capable of so much – it was very inspiring.

Helen asked us to come out on another ride while we were there and thought it was a great opportunity to have some fun. One of the travellers came out on the ride with us, along with a couple of other people. This time, we went on different tracks. Helen separated Russell and me in parts and stopped and asked me how to get her horse to climb a rock and stand with just its front feet on it. To this day, I'm not sure if she hadn't done this before and was testing me, or whether she wanted a real lesson. I could tell she had skills, a lot more than me in some areas. Russell and I sat on our horses, and I talked Helen through how to work with her horse for individual foot control. It only took a couple of minutes and she had achieved what she wanted. She told me that she'd been trying to do that for a long time but both she and her horse would always just get frustrated. She told me I made it easy and was thankful. This meant a lot from someone like Helen.

We continued the track, then Helen stopped and asked her other rider to stay back with the others and just walk and catch up with us, she then turned to me and said come with me. We then proceeded to canter off on a single trail, weaving this way and that, following the trail, with Helen squealing with laughter like a child and yelling, 'Two crazy ladies riding through the bush.' I laughed with her as we cantered along the trail, thinking how much fun it was. Raw, stupid, fun. We stopped after what seemed like quite a distance and the beaming grin on Helen's face said it all – she loved her horses. She explained how she never got to do that, as she must always have the horses contained and quiet because most people who go out on the trails can't ride. She told me how much fun it was to have people who could ride with her for a change and also told me that she hoped we would continue to visit her property in the future.

It was something that I felt sure would happen. When the rest of the group caught up with us, Russell could see the pure joy on my face.

On the last day we were staying at Helen's she had the mares, foals and Captain in the yards. Helen hadn't done any liberty work riding. She had worked with the foals a lot at liberty to get them used to people though. She explained she had never tried any liberty riding. She asked how I rode at liberty. I explained I just used my hands or at most a small soft string under the horse's neck. Most of the communication was done through your body. She asked if I could jump on Captain and show her. I asked whether he was fine to ride, and she assured me he was good. There would normally be a lot of preparing groundwork I would do with a horse first before doing this, but I trusted Helen and we were in a contained yard. I jumped on straight away, amongst the mares and foals, with just a string around his neck. Captain was calm and relaxed, and it was obvious he was safe and at home with his wives and kids around him. I could tell he had some buttons on him, but it was obvious that he hadn't worked this way before. He was new to this but responsive and it didn't take much to get a few things happening. What a great opportunity. He was a magnificent-natured stallion. When I jumped off after a few minutes Helen said he did well, as no one had done anything like that with him before, which was lovely to hear.

Russell and I at our first trip to Helen's

At night at Helen's place, Russell and I would just sit on our balcony and watch the herd of mares, foals and Captain. We learnt so much by watching the herd and how they worked together. It was fascinating. The morning we left, Helen came to say goodbye and we could tell she enjoyed having us there as much as we enjoyed being there. Both Russell and I felt we had just found our happy place to be during those difficult times when we couldn't have our kids with us.

Helen and I with Bella at Angler's Rest

16

Life as a trainer

I continued to work as much as I could when I didn't have my kids. I was giving a lot more horsemanship lessons – both on the ground and riding. I was also doing my own clinics with clients, which felt normal to me. I found I was starting to see things immediately and that I instinctively felt I knew how to help. I started being able to feel when horses were sore and work out the line of when things were behavioural, physical, or both.

I had built a good support network of other professionals so that I could help horses and people with holistic care. Great vets, farriers, and bodyworkers. The more clinics I did, the more fun I had. I would give themed clinics and games days and tried to incorporate the fun of learning into what I was trying to teach and share with others. Ruth helped me in the first few years by providing catered morning teas, lunches and afternoon teas that were becoming more popular than my training. Things were getting busier fast.

I still wasn't professionally starting other people's horses, but that was about to change. The client who had lost their six-year-old mare contacted me, as they had been given a free thoroughbred mare that was unstarted, and she wanted it for her daughter. I explained that I didn't think a green horse was a good idea for a teenage girl, however, I did believe this girl was different. She had a quiet, understanding demeanour about her and I felt they would have done this with or without me. Her mum asked if I would be willing to start this mare for her. I explained I normally don't do this for clients, and she put up a convincing argument about why I should. Thanks for that. You know who you are. I had probably worked with over one thousand horses by that time and starting them under saddle for others did seem like a natural progression. The mare was dropped off at my property soon after. She was a chestnut mare – a five-year-old thoroughbred that was 15.2hh. If my memory is correct, someone had sat on her and possibly led her a few steps but nothing else. I find this doesn't really help and often makes horses harder to start. Her name was Tramp. She was a nice type of mare and relatively easy to start. Back then, I did generally start them as much as I could under saddle within six to eight weeks. I was particular about their body strength, posture and how long I was on their back – and had learnt how to look after them physically and mentally to ensure I was doing the absolute best I could do.

I was very proud of the start I did with Tramp and when it came to giving her back to the owner, I insisted her daughter rode her and handled her for a week before leaving. I had always made it a condition of working with people's horses that they were part of the process so that they understood the journey and the language that their horse understood. I would always do the high-risk work but, being my first professional start, I did hold off on a teenage girl jumping on too soon. *I have now learnt that it is vital to get the owner on within the first three sits and rides from a trust and bonding experience.* I had the owner's daughter working exceptionally well with her horse with groundwork and liberty on the ground and the riding was slow but steady. I could ride this mare softly at walk, trot or canter, as well as deal with opening and shutting gates and doing obstacles. She was always soft and relaxed. The owner would ride her, and although the walk and trot were pretty good, the transition from trot to canter was always risky, with the mare feeling pressured and wanting to either pig root or let out a minor buck. The owner was not at the same level of riding as me and not as soft, but I thought the mare could have coped.

This continued for a few sessions and it got me thinking that I could only start horses for myself successfully – not for others. I rang my mentor Ben and explained everything to him. Once he had politely listened to me, he kindly said that this was great for a first professional start, now go back and fix the horse for the level the owner is at. That made sense. I needed to numb and desensitise the horse for a more unbalanced rougher rider. Ben confirmed and said that once they are both confident with each other, then soften them up. That man was wise beyond his years.

I spent another week with Tramp and rode rough and sloppy until the horse was confident with this new style. The day then came when I needed to put the owner back on. The teenager was a good horsewoman and rider for her age, but this just happened to be a chestnut thoroughbred mare she was dealing with, so need I say more? *For those that are non-horsey, this type of horse has a reputation for being difficult and hot-headed.* When the owner got on, she went to canter and it was smooth and consistent. I am sure Tramp was thinking, 'This kid is a way better rider than what this lady has been doing lately. I'm sticking with her.' These two went on to have an amazing relationship. This mare had her quirks, but the owner managed them beautifully and they have done lots over the years together. This experience changed how I worked with clients and horses for starting. The owner had to start getting on earlier, even if they didn't move, or if the horse just followed me at liberty, with the owner on within the first few rides after I knew the horse was confident. I worked solidly with the horse but always made the comfort and the end of a big session with the owner finishing. Horses remember the last thing you did before releasing pressure or putting them away. By always getting the owner to ask the last thing before turning a horse back out into the paddock their loyalty became stronger with the owner. I felt this helped with the transition of the owner taking them home.

***

Russell and I decided to get a puppy. We were now living together on the property and had been together for almost three years. He had owned kelpies before and was keen on one, so that's what we got. Matilda, or Mattie for short. Yes, I know we already have a horse called this, but I love the name. My first ASH was Matilda, and now our first kelpie together was Matilda. She was a red kelpie and, although we didn't know it at the time, as she was the same size as all the other puppies, she was the runt of the litter. Matilda was like our first child together. She came everywhere with us. I had never owned a kelpie before and was amazed at how easy she was to train. One thing I did pick up is that you get almost only one chance to get it right and it must be right from the start. For example, we don't lock our dogs up – we let them have the whole property to roam but they are not allowed to cross over a border fence. The first time Matilda went to do this I growled at her and that was enough for her to cower. We trained her around every fence of the whole property and she never crossed that imaginary line. With other things like the mower, I never told her no for the first few times when we used it, so she began to herd the mower when we were on it. Once she had the game on for herding, we weren't going to change her mind. We were both smitten with her. She had been locked in a dirt pen before we got her and didn't know anything else. When we first got her home, we let her out onto some grass and she walked like a puppet. To us, she was perfect.

I had also started Chika. We had our first rides when he was four and a half. He was a very easy start. He was 15.2hh and had a great build. By the time a year had passed since I started him, he was becoming very handy. It was 2011, and he was five years old. Due to work commitments, he was fast becoming my main horse. Matilda was still with us and was a great riding horse but as she was in her teens, I lightened her load a bit. She was now the old, reliable one.

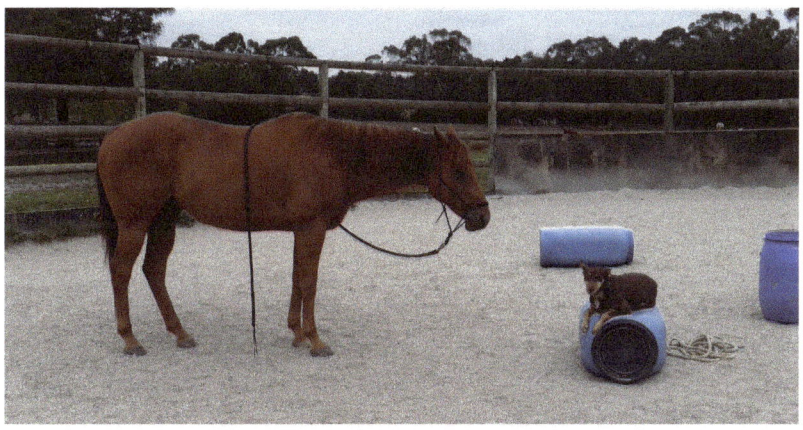

Chika and Matilda, our dog

Both Yella and Koko's foals were due. Koko foaled first with no complications and finally gave us a jet-black filly. She was stunning. Because she was so fluffy and black and seemed to be all legs, she looked like a giant huntsman. We named her Panuk, which means 'better'. She was another baby Russell and I felt we had. After giving birth to her, Koko showed signs of mild colic while trying to pass the placenta. Koko had done this with every foal and, to stop vets coming out in the middle of the night, they were now comfortable with me giving her a dose of 'bute' (Phenylbutazone, common prescription non-steroidal anti-inflammatory used to reduce inflammation and pain relief). This managed her symptoms with each birth and helped her feel comfortable. I had an instant attraction to Panuk. I have a thing for mares. She was perfect in my eyes and, because she had very high leg carriage and lift, she looked exceptional when she moved. She was a very placid-natured horse. We thought we had won Tattslotto.

Three weeks later, Yella had her first foal with us. I had a very dear client who wanted a horse from a foal to buy and we couldn't keep both foals. When Yella was foaling, I let the client know, so she could be part of the birth experience. I can't remember exactly if she made it in time or just after the birth, as things got a bit scary. I had our normal cheat notes from uni to monitor the birthing process and Yella was struggling in the final part of the delivery. You know when your horse is in trouble when she comes over to you in labour and pushes her stomach on you and looks back. Yella made some very weird noises and went from me to Russell pleading for help. She put her back end right on Russell and started to back into him. It was heart-wrenching. I was just about to call the vet when Russell said to allow her one more contraction. With that we saw the first hoof appear, then the next and a nose. Although very aggressive with contractions, the foal was born. A palomino colt. It was lovely to share and educate a client with everything from birth, she helped us time and document all milestones post-birth to ensure everything was considered normal. Yella held on to the placenta the next day, which I knew was considered a complication and so, although all other milestones were being met by the mare and foal, we needed veterinary assistance.

When the vet arrived, he was confident it would only take one hit of oxytocin and another hour for the placenta to be dispelled, but it didn't work. It took three visits and further medications as well as gentle internal manipulation. The vet said it was the most difficult removal he had experienced. I relayed my concern that this could be a sign of something wrong with the foal but he dispelled my concerns, as everything else was normal. The colt continued to flourish, and we were confident he was going to be amazing. We debated whether to keep him instead of Panuk, but my heart was already set on my girl. The client advised she would like to buy the colt and be part of his training going forward, as it was a unique opportunity to learn handling right from the start. We agreed. We looked up several names and let the client decide on his name. She picked Ku which meant 'give'. I thought it was perfect. The client who bought him was amazing and worked with us under instruction to give him the best handling we thought he could get. They created a great bond with each other. It was lovely to watch.

When Panuk turned six weeks old and was due for worming, I got a little concerned. I did lots of handling of all our foals and could always catch them, lead them with my arms cradling them, file their feet, worm them and brush them – all with no halter and with them very relaxed. I went to worm her with a worming tube, the same way I do all the foals and horses. Her head went up, which is normal. They usually raise their head a little but settle soon after when they relax. I had previously practised with my finger in her mouth and done all other pre-work, so was surprised at what happened next. Once her head went up, she seemed to startle herself and ran backwards. This was exactly what her mum Koko had done – and still did! – every time I wormed her. I had started using another vet and rang him that afternoon to explain the situation. He politely listened and then confirmed everything at the end. In short, he said most people struggle to worm a foal, let alone catch them and handle everything without a halter on. I halter trained her the next week and when she was due to be wormed again, I had the same response. I talked to several people about this, thinking there must be something to it. Why would her mum and her both do it? I was told by several people that I see too much. Don't overthink it. Don't look for excuses. But I felt it was very unusual, and I felt they were trying to tell me something.

***

Over the next few years, I worked exceptionally hard and got a bit of a local reputation for working out difficult horses. I would attend as many of my clients' veterinary consults as I could when things weren't right to continue to educate myself. I started to have a horse chiropractor and bodyworker work from our property where he would work with up to ten horses on the days he came, which ended up being once a month.

***

I had just done a beach clinic with some dear friends – a mother and daughter – who had become clients. I was giving the daughter a private lesson on liberty work, as she was very interested. She was another talented young lady that I enjoyed working with. Very clever, savvy and put the time in. She was also heart and soul. I was just explaining some traits I commonly saw in horses when she turned and said, 'That sounds like the Little Albert experiment.' She was studying psychology and said they had discussed it at university.

I was explaining a pattern of things I sometimes see with horses that have triggers that set them off in fear. She explained this famous experiment and how it sounded familiar.

The Little Albert experiment was first conducted in the 1920s by two psychologists showing evidence of classical conditioning in humans. To bastardise it into a summary, these psychologists (Watson & Rayner) performed a study on a nine-month-old boy to determine if classical conditioning worked on humans as well as animals. They took the Russian physiologist, Ivan Pavlov's experiments that he had shown on dogs and applied them to a human. The experiment is today known as very controversial, and the boy was pulled out of the experiment before conclusions could be drawn or reversed. In short, they trained this infant to negatively react to the colour white or fluffy animals. Whenever white or fluffy objects were presented, they would make a loud noise and by day five of the experiment the boy was brought to tears by a white rat, rabbit, Santa Clause mask, and even his own pets. I could go on and on about this but just google to see the full information as it is now seen to have been an unethical study that unnecessarily traumatised an innocent child for life in the name of science. Like everything on the internet, there are varying details, but you'll get the meaning.

I often refer clients to this experiment so I can emphasise, from a human perspective, how many horses have triggers from accidents or bad handling. Personally, if I hear some mobile phone notification noises that I have had previously during a certain time of my life, I can hear the noise and instantly feel dread, fear and physical illness. From a horse perspective, I can recall a client's horse that I worked with to restart. Ted was a bay gelding quarter horse that was roughly eight years old. He came to us very fearful, and difficult to catch, float and ride. I worked with him for a few weeks and we had some great things going. By the end of that time, Ted would always come to me or wait and stand to be caught, and he was relaxed and respectful loading, unloading, and travelling on a float. Best of all, he had changed completely with riding, from almost trembling to willing and calm. Don't get me wrong – it wasn't all simple. There was bodywork, ulcer treatments, saddle fitting and more that all had to be done during the process but, again, I was incredibly pleased with the result. It was a few days before the owner was coming to collect him when I went out early in the morning to bring him in. It was an incredibly cold morning and I rarely wear gloves but this morning I did. I picked up Ted's halter and walked down to his paddock where he saw me, neighed and began to walk toward me. Just as he got to me, I rubbed him on his neck before putting the halter up, when he suddenly snorted, looked at my hands and then flew backwards and bolted off.

It took me half an hour before he would stop running and calm down. I took the gloves off thinking this may be the cause. I worked with him for some time at liberty and he finally relaxed enough to stand and face up to me and allow me to approach. When I was at his shoulder, he stared at my hands, sniffed them and snorted. I just stood for a few minutes and slowly rubbed his neck again. When I went to walk off, he followed me and exhaled out like he had survived a run for his life. To double prove my theory, the next day I left the pair of gloves on the ground in the paddock where Ted couldn't see. I then did join up with him at liberty and got him to follow me without any equipment so I knew he could react freely if needed. We then walked casually across the paddock, and I felt our trust was back. I then casually walked just next to the gloves on the ground, which Ted almost stood on, and then he baulked, snorted and jumped away from them. He ran a little way away from me and just watched. I did some join-up work with him to get him to face me from a distance and watch me. I then walked back to the gloves and picked them up from the ground. His head rose in anticipation and he watched, ready to react. I then walked away with the gloves and threw them over the fence – as far away as possible. I then went back to Ted and got him to join up and come to me. He dropped his head in my hands as if to say 'thank you'.

I rang the owner that afternoon to explain and thought she was going to think I was making excuses for him. I explained everything was still great, but that I thought someone had previously hurt Ted while wearing gloves, so to be aware of it, as I believed it was a trigger and that some triggers never leave, as too much damage sometimes has been done. I was not saying to not work with the horse to change his thoughts and feelings about gloves, but to note this was a trigger and she needed to be aware and work with this. The owner then burst out crying. She told me that both of her previous trainers had used gloves, and she couldn't work out why she would send him to a trainer and he would come back worse. Neither of us will ever know what happened but now that the owner was aware, she could use this information to both their benefits. I am not saying previous trainers were the cause, but that someone had worn gloves or used gloves to cause this reaction. It could have just been an accident; we will never know. The last time I heard, they were working great together, and the owner felt their trust and relationship were at the best level she could imagine. I love my job sometimes.

Within the same year, I experienced similar responses by two horses to baseball hats. The hats being the cause and hence the trigger, which once identified, could be worked on to lessen the reaction to it. I found the biggest learning was from their response the following day. I could work with a horse that was scared or triggered by a hat, and within an hour have me and the horse wearing it, rubbing it, and throwing it everywhere, with them being perfectly calm. The big difference was the following day. If they picked up from where I left them the previous day with training, I was not concerned. If it was Groundhog Day and you had to go through an hour of work again, this always concerned me. I have seen, when this happens, that either the horse has mental health issues from the previous trauma to the degree of PTSD or there is a physical reason for it. Either way, both ways require lots of understanding and investigation.

    Don't get me wrong, some of the horses I have seen with this are brilliant in every other way, there is just a major trigger that you need to be aware of, work with and be understanding and empathetic to. The biggest two examples of extremes I can think of around that time were very different from each other. One was clearly PTSD, the other was a physical issue. The first horse was owned by an amazing Australian trainer. I attended one of his clinics and, of all the clinics I had attended – and there were a lot – I got the most from him. This trainer knew what I did for a job and was so generous and supportive with his advice and time. He let me either work or ride three of his best horses. Not many people will allow you this opportunity, but he was so focused on everyone learning. One of his horses, who I had seen at Equitana doing an amazing demonstration, had issues with rugs. His honesty in sharing the horse's story was such a great teaching tool and example. This trainer had been given this horse and, on the day he arrived, the trainer put a rug on him. The horse didn't seem to mind, so the trainer left it on him for the night.

    That night, there was a terrible thunderstorm. The next morning, when he found his new horse, it was two paddocks down with the rug barely on. This stunning horse, who I had seen this trainer ride at liberty doing flying lead changes, slide stops and lying down, had his own issue with rugs. It had been five years since that accident and the trainer showed us how his horse was still wary of the rug every day. He went on to explain he had worked with this horse almost daily for years to try to fix this, and every time he would get him to accept it and relax, but it still took time and patience every day.

If, even at their level, they still had this complication to struggle with, I think the rest of us need to cut ourselves and our horses some slack.

The other case was way more complex. A good friend who was also a client ended up with a rescue horse that had been running with a herd when the RSPCA got involved and all horses were surrendered. This horse had lots of issues and was sore all over and very nervous. For the safety of the horse and us, even though I worked with this horse for some time, we sedated the horse to float it back to our property. *I was always against sedating for transport, but now that I'm more experienced and have had to use a fair bit, if the training is right and the sedation used correctly with it, I think it is a much safer and better way to deal with some situations and prevents the horse having a further negative experience.* I worked with this horse for a few weeks. Gypsy. She was always hard to catch, always nervous to be touched and I would have to run through the same issues every day. I would go to catch her; I would have to take my time and be very careful and talk on my approach. I would put her halter on, walk her back, groom her and then do some groundwork. Things only ever got mildly better – even though I had been trimming her feet, her teeth had been done and she was wormed and getting treatment for stomach ulcers. Despite all that handling, she still had so many triggers that I knew there had to be something more. Her issues were systemic. After a week or so, I started climbing on her bareback with a halter and had her very relaxed by the end of the session. I could climb on and off and rub her all over and she was in love with me by the end of the session. But the next day I got her out, it was Groundhog Day again. This went on for a week. I explained to the owner that I didn't think we could go any further. I explained I would keep going a bit longer to try to find some answers but didn't like my chances.

At that time, I had been starting another horse, Denzel. He was a five-year-old brown quarter-horse. He was 15.2hh and a beautiful boy. A very dear client who had given me several of her horses to start had bred him and wanted me to start him and find him another home, as she didn't have time to ride him – and she knew he was something special. He was ... and still is. I would probably put Denzel in my top ten for best horses I have ridden. Ever! His nature was the best. To give you an idea of what his nature was like when I was brushing him one day before a ride, I noticed he was picking up one back leg. He would pick it up and just turn and look back. I was thinking, crap, don't tell me he has colic or something. About the fifth time he did this, I noticed the bottom of his tail moving. I then grabbed his tail and noticed it was too heavy for just a tail. I then pulled from the middle of his tail our new kitten I had just got for Mother's Day. I removed the kitten and put it a few metres away. But the kitten had other ideas and thought, 'Great game' ... then bolted back to her tail hiding spot and jumped back in. Denzel calmly just lifted one foot again and looked back. To help solve the problem, I thought I was smart and I tied a knot in Denzel's tail, so it was out of the way. But the kitten just bolted straight to the leg he had been raising and grabbed hold of his fetlock and did a bouncy dance around it. Denzel simply just lifted his foot again and held it up to make sure he didn't hurt this feral fur ball. Kitten? Three. Me? Zero. I then put the kitten inside the house. This kitten was called Smudge and almost became one.

Now you know Denzel's temperament. I decided to watch how he was with Gypsy, as I couldn't work it out. They had been in the paddock the whole time together and they always seemed very relaxed and calm. I started to pay more attention.

The very next day I got my answer. I honestly cannot remember what frightened them, but something happened and all the horses started running in the back paddocks. Probably a rogue kangaroo or deer. I straight away turned to watch Gypsy and Denzel, being clients' horses, to make sure they were ok and noticed what I had been missing all along. Denzel was herding Gypsy away from fences and obstacles. She couldn't see. The vet confirmed she had issues in both eyes and would have the effect of a Kaleidoscope on her vision. Gypsy would be seeing lots of confusing images in parts. This type of change in their eyes can be caused by an STD, and, considering she had been running with a stallion and it looked like she may have had a foal before, this made sense. There was no way of fixing this and the condition of confusing vision is scarier to a horse than being blind. The owner and I decided the best and kindest thing to do was euthanasia. Gypsy was given a lethal injection and, after she passed, the vet noticed a huge tumour emerge from her vulva. There was no point in doing a biopsy, but it was more than likely cancer. That poor mare! What a life and what an amazing horse to have still tried so hard with all she had going on. What an amazing person she finally ended up with who did everything they could to get an answer.

On another note, once Denzel had been started, I contacted one of our clients who was and still is one of our closest friends and told them they had to buy this horse, and so they did – for their daughter. Wasn't that a great decision! He is spoiled rotten and they have an amazing life together.

I was finding that, as a trainer, you had to know a lot more than just how to physically train a horse. You also had to be aware of when things were not going to plan. You had to work out whether it was behavioural, or pain related. When I got horses that no one had messed with and had no physical issues, they were so easy to train. It was like, as they say, taking candy from a baby. This just solidified, more and more, the importance of understanding the line of when things were not right.

Chika and I working horses in Starting Clinic

Koko and Panuk

Starting Clydesdale, Harry from Chika

Starting Hoss at Beach Clinic

Training Swassis to trust

Chika and I going for a dip during a Clinic

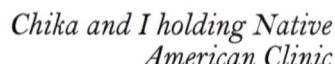

Chika and I holding Native American Clinic

Swassis and I another Native American Clinic

Chika and I starting Clinic

Bella and I holding Beach Clinic

Bella and I at another Beach Clinic

Liberty demonstration with Bella at Clinic

17

My big teachers

Panuk and Ku were now a year old. It was 2012. Ku was doing well with his new owner but it had become noticeable in the last few months that he always grazed with his left leg forward. He had also been mildly lame once on that same foot. We worked with the farrier to try to assist him in balancing and using a variation of feeding methods. That is, put hay nets, and hard feed at certain heights to simulate a more natural environment and get him to spend more time with his weight spread equally across all his legs.

Panuk was a doll. A stunningly elegant-looking filly, with a deep connection with us. I had a minor concern still with her behaviour with a couple of things; it was not making sense. She still looked a little high-gaited to me as far as she seemed to lift her legs high for her breed. I still had several people saying I see too much, but everyone has their quirks. This was different. Don't get me wrong, I questioned myself majorly too. I kept thinking I couldn't have it all. That little voice in my head that had been through so much trauma was wary. I had two beautiful sons and a loving partner and work was going great. Did we just breed my dream horse? Was I just used to having trauma?

Ku and Panuk as foals asleep

***

I met a new client who had brought her horse across from America with her and was having some behavioural changes. We started working together and shared lots of similarities with USA-based trainers we admired. We worked together well, and she moved her horse to our property while she stayed in Australia. Her husband had been asked to come to Australia for work for two years. We built an amazing bond and worked through some things with her horse. It was also a great learning experience for me to have a local's knowledge on tap of how things are done with horses in the States. We formed a great friendship.

***

I began working more with Giha. At that stage, he was turning five years old and was probably to date the best-looking horse we had bred. His face had recovered from his accident when he was a foal and, as far as we could tell, there were no long-term issues except the scars from the stitches on his head. He was a dark liver chestnut, 15.3hh, with a big strong build. The concern I had with him since working with him from a yearling was that there seemed to be a dramatic reaction to any fright. To give you an example, something would jump out and he would shy, but it was way bigger than most horses I came across. I couldn't work it out. I do a lot of groundwork over the years before I start riding any of our horses and, generally, when you get on them for the first time, they are half-asleep. Giha was different.

My biggest concern was that, when working him on the ground, he would drop a hind leg at the canter. It didn't improve with strengthening work or with rest. It was always there. I had several vets do assessments on him and none could answer what it was. I kept getting told it was a strength thing, work him more. But that wasn't working. The other thing that was obvious was a hypersensitivity to needles. Again, when his head went up, he was difficult to handle and became angry. The number of people who kept telling me it was a training issue when, with all due respect, I had trained more horses than them. From a behaviour point of view, I was also more experienced, but that lack of confidence in me made me listen to other people's thoughts.

With the pressure of being a trainer, money and the fact that we had bred this horse, I continued to start him and began riding him. One thought was that this could be a hangover from his accident when he was a foal, but nothing obvious, physically. I honestly felt that this odd behaviour and dropping a leg was there before the accident but that it had gradually got worse over the last few years.

Giha was a big, powerful unit. I probably had maybe ten hours riding on him. Russell and I went out on a trail one day when the weather was calm and sunny. Russell was riding Chika, who was our most reliable horse at that time. Giha was going along nicely, a little nervous but nothing major. I needed to get him off the gravel road we were riding on and do a step up onto the verge where there was more room. The step up was not huge, it was about the height of his knees. As soon as we stepped up Giha turned his head slightly and did a massive buck, so I came off. I got thrown a metre or two and lay on the ground winded for a bit. Again, it was a massive reaction to nothing, really. Afterwards, Giha just looked down on me, relaxed and quiet as if to say, 'What happened?'

I continued to work with Giha and the bodyworker I had at that time said he was very tight at the base of the neck and chest, and injected him to help. I also started using an ultrasound machine with horses, which helped. I was trained on it by one of the bodyworkers who was extensively experienced and worked with vets. I started treating horses with the ultrasound machine after he had assessed them. It was great for me to feel horses before, then treat them and then feel them after. Their bodies were teaching me. I have probably used the ultrasound machine on about 100 horses now and find it a valuable tool when combined with other treatments and, of course, correct training.

I started using the ultrasound machine a lot and found it very useful to soften muscles on our horses and help keep Chika and Giha more relaxed for riding. Chika would also get tight in the same spots as Giha, but never to the same degree.

I had put some more hours on Giha in the round yard and arena trying to build strength and get us better together with lateral work thinking it could only help. Not only was I trying to build strength and flexibility but get him more accustomed to giving his whole body to me with collection work, which I feel is not just a physical thing but a psychological partnership. Russell and I decided to take both Chika and Giha out for a ride and take Mattie, our dog with us.

Mattie was such a brilliant dog and so easy to train. So well-behaved. We were riding down a narrow track and everything seemed to be going well. I was in front, then Russell on Chika and Mattie at the back. If we asked her to stay behind, she would stay behind the last horse. We got to a slightly wider part of the track and Russell said to Mattie, 'Up front.' Thinking the track was wider on the right, I put my right leg on Giha to bend his ribs away and have his head slightly to the right to see Mattie coming and give her room to pass. I was feeling confident our lateral work had paid off. Then Mattie ran past on the other side, the left.

Giha bent his head slightly back to the left and, as I realised she was coming to the other side, I went to change legs to make room for her and it was too late. Giha exploded. It was a huge overreaction and buck again. I was thrown high and landed heavy on one side. I was winded again and it took about ten minutes before I could move. Once I got up, I crawled back on, yelping as I did. We rode back to the property with Mattie up front and me holding myself. Something felt wrong, I just didn't know what. Once we got home, Russell took care of the horses, and I went inside and took some pain relief and anti-inflammatory. I waited a bit, and the pain wasn't changing. I rang Nurse on-Call and chatted with them and they advised me to get to a hospital, as it could be internal injuries. I said I would be fine, but asked about what things I should look out for. They told me the list of possible ailments could include further pain, blood in my urine, blurry vision, etc.

An hour went by and the next time I went to the toilet, I was bleeding. We drove to the hospital where I stayed for the night under supervision, and they checked everything out. I had bruised my kidneys, apparently. Didn't know that was a thing. It subsided by the morning, so I was discharged. It was hard to move but when I got home, I got Giha out immediately. It was a windy day, and I knew these were the days he was at his worst. I really needed to work out what was going on as no one was helping me. I had no intention of getting on him, and truth be known, I probably didn't have the physical strength, but I led him down the driveway. At the end of our driveway near the road we have large cypress trees where it can be a little scary for horses as it is like a large tunnel. As I predicted, when I walked Giha to the start of the trees a bird flew out which was enough for him to do his over-exaggeration shy where he then did a massive buck. It was like watching it in slow motion. When the bird startled him, he tried to do a small movement sideways, but one of his hind legs got left behind so he pushed as hard as he could with the other three legs to buck. Mid-air, it was like he worked out where his other hind leg was and then put it in the right position to land. He couldn't help it. His brain couldn't talk to all four feet at once. He was neurologically impaired.

I decided that, at the ripe old age of six years old, he was to be retired. A week later, I got on him one last time in the round yard. I just did a tiny walk and stopped and bent over his neck while on him. I threw my arms around his neck and just cried into his mane for five minutes or more. Time stood still. We both knew this was the last time anyone would try to ride him, and I am sure he understood and was grateful. It was the quietest he had been. Giha was now a paddock ornament as we like to call them once retired. It would break our hearts looking at him as he was such a beautiful horse physically and mentally, but we knew we had made the right decision.

***

We had trouble getting Koko pregnant again and, after getting vets involved, tried a few things but decided it wasn't meant to be, so stopped putting her to Java. She had now had four foals for us: Chika, Giha, Takota and Panuk. Yella was pregnant again and gave birth to a very active chestnut colt with a big white blaze. It was the spring of 2013. The birth went better than her birth with Ku and, considering her previous placenta retention, the vet had given me some Oxytocin to inject shortly after she foaled. This worked perfectly and she passed the placenta this time, no issues. This colt was full of beans and ridiculously friendly. We called him Oniwa, which means 'can't stand still'. His nickname was Oni. He really was a character. From the time he was born, you could be at the other side of the paddock and call him and, no matter what he was doing, he would run flat out up to you for attention. He was special.

18

Doing the miles

We continued to go to Helen's at least once a year, if not more often. Angler's Rest had become like our second home. We took friends there and stayed several different times and even held one of our client's Christmas parties there. We used to always have a few days away with horses in January or some sort of other big event to say thank you to clients for trusting us with their horses and themselves. Russell and I decided to buy one of Helen's horses to start and take home. I wanted to see the difference in these horses from their upbringing. We had gone up two months earlier to have a look and I had my eye on a little blue roan mare called Bella. She was six years old, 14.2hh and gorgeous looking, besides a dent in her forehead and one slightly twisted foot. She had the best temperament and nature. One of the softest horses I had met.

Russell and I were pretty sure we would buy her but wanted to just have another look. We had about ten clients with us for this Xmas party at Helen's; it was January 2015. We all had a drink in our hand and were looking over the fence chatting while we looked at the herd Bella was in. She was in with another 25 odd horses. Someone asked which horse I was keen on. I pointed her out - she was right up the back of the herd. I called, 'Bella, Bella,' and her ears popped up. I then turned away and started chatting to everyone, not seeing what was happening. Just as I was explaining we weren't 100 per cent on our decision to get her, everyone started sniggering and staring at the horse herd. I turned around and Bella was parting the herd and pushing the others out the way until she was right at the fence next to us. She looked me straight in the eye. Sold. She chose us.

Client Xmas party at Helen's

Bella at Helen's

Two weeks later, we went back to Helen's with a float and brought Bella home. I worked with her for a few days to float train her. We then took her for a test drive up the road with me in the float. She was ok, and starting to become very attached to me. We floated her back home, where she pawed the float for the first 30 minutes of the trip. When this behaviour got her nowhere, she just went quiet. It took us another six hours to get home. We didn't let her out for a break as we should have after three hours as it was too risky. Two people had tried to start riding Bella previously and she had reared on both of the riders. Since then, she had really had no further work done with her. We got her home with no incidents and she came off the float slowly. She was a thinker. I gave her electrolytes and put her in our foaling paddock, which was secure, but no electric fencing. We have concrete troughs, which was a bit like an alien to her. It probably took her another couple of hours before she ventured to the trough to have a well-deserved drink. Once she did start to drink, I noticed she just stood with her head above the trough for hours. She would eat hay and grass but no hard feed. The next morning, she was still standing above the trough and moving her head slightly. I started panicking, thinking we had given her brain damage or something. When I walked up close and watched her, she was playing with the water. She would have a mouthful of water and then gently stick her tongue out with her teeth on either side of it. Then occasionally she would spray a bit of water through her front teeth and draw little pictures on top of the trough water surface. She was a funny girl. Obviously, this water surface was quite different from the dams and rivers she was used to drinking from.

Bella's mum was a brumby, and her dad was Captain, who was half-Friesian and half-quarter horse. She was very soft and intelligent. I finished starting her and she became a brilliant riding horse. If she was a hand bigger, she would have been my perfect riding horse. Gorgeous in presence and so willing to please.

I continued to work with any horses there that were thrown at me to help Helen whenever we were at the property. Everyone we took there had the same amazing response we had to the property and Helen. Mattie our kelpie loved it there. We went to Helen's a couple of times with my two boys and stayed in the cabins, which were probably not quite what they enjoyed. Liam got sick both times, and we suspect it was from the water. We began to always take our own drinking water and that seemed to sort that out.

One of the most memorable times at Helen's was when we had some close friends with us staying there. We were all sitting on deck chairs in front of the cabins having a drink and watching Captain with his herd of mares. There had been a new mare introduced to the herd a few days earlier and it looked like she was coming into season. I don't know whether she was a maiden mare or not, but she wasn't having a bar of Captain's advances. He was hounding the new mare and was using the tactic of, 'I will eventually wear you down'. Another mare was standing back and watching and when Captain got more intense, she intervened. We assumed this was the lead mare in the herd and she must have thought, back off big fella, let her feel her own way. Now, as far as I understood in a herd, the lead mare did discipline within the herd, and drove the herd for food and water, etc. The stallion is purely for procreation and protection. What we then witnessed showed that, if a stallion thinks a mare is right for serving, this attitude trumps the lead mare, big time.

The new mare scattered away as the older matriarch of the herd cut her away from Captain. Captain then turned his attention to the mare that had intervened. The look in a stallion's eye when you have made them angry is very intense. It's not the same look as when they feel threatened or need to protect and feel they must kill or injure. It's the look of, 'you made me do this; to stand my ground and keep my credibility, there will be consequences'. It is very raw and quite full-on. Captain now charged the matriarch mare and ran her. He hunted her up and down a dam wall, around and around and it was obvious he was fitter and stronger. The mare was kicking back trying to deter him while she ran, but he was too experienced for this to have any effect. This is the first time I really understood why horses move their heads in what I describe it as 'snaking'. It is when a horse drops their head as low as it can go to the ground and tilt their jaw up. It creates a hollow spot above the ground and their head. When they do this, they can still closely pursue their target and not get kicked. Captain continued to hunt the matriarch mare down for what seemed like 30 minutes or more.

We were planning to go to the pub for tea that night but none of us could move; it was the best movie we had ever watched. We took it in turns for one of us to run in and out of the cabin to get drinks and nibbles, as none of us wanted to miss out on the story unfolding in front of us. The matriarch mare was exhausted, heaving as she was out of breath. Captain turned away from her and went back to the new mare. The matriarch watched, but didn't move. Within minutes Captain was serving the new mare while the other mare just watched on. Over the next couple of hours, we watched Captain move around the rest of the herd with his new mare, covering her several more times while the matriarch moved out the way.

The next morning, when we got up and walked out of the cabin, which was in a small valley, Captain and the new mare stood next to each other at the top of the hill, the matriarch mare at the base of the hill below them and in front of the rest of the herd. Want to learn how horses think? Watch them in this forum, horse psychology 101. Best learning ground ever.

I started riding Takota as he was now a five-year-old. He was great fun, sensitive, brave, and very willing. Normally, I would ride all our starters for most of the first year, but as Takota was going to be Russell's horse, I got him to finish the starting process. Their personalities were well matched, and they complemented each other. Russell was chilled and didn't interfere with horses when they were going well. Takota could get a bit pumped and shied a lot more than your average horse. Russell blamed himself a little for this, saying that because none of the others were like this, it must have been his work with him. I don't believe that at all. Takota had similar issues to his siblings with the base of his neck always getting tight and although not needle shy or reacting strongly when his head was in the air, there was still a sensitivity. A lot of people say traits run in genetic lines; this was still not making sense to me.

With all the horses I handled for clients, I could feel ours were more respectful and had the desire to try to please us in them, but a few things just didn't add up. Was it my training? Was the common factor in a couple of these odd traits me? Don't get me wrong, Takota was still a brilliant riding horse.

***

Life seemed to be flying along. The kids kept us busy when they were with us and, when they weren't, I was working big hours. I got a couple more horses and was quicker at working out their behaviour issues were due to sight impairments. Now I mentally had a tick sheet for training horses. Ones without major physical issues but still had minor 'white rabbits' became so easy. Starting and training these horses was an absolute joy. The ones that weren't like this I just kept working with and investigating until we had answers.

***

In one year, I had two horses I nicknamed 'flippers'. Both these horses came to me for training, as they had reared and flipped over on their owners when under pressure and from contact with the bit in their mouth. Both supposedly had dental work checked on their mouths to eliminate teeth as a cause. One even had the invoice from another trainer with the charge on it for a dental. Now, I am not going to try to rant too much but a lay dentist being someone who is not a qualified vet, in my view, has no right to do dental work on horses' mouths. In the human world, we wouldn't allow someone in our mouths without some very clear medical background, yet some still think it is ok for a horse. Yes, back in the 1980s it was different. But now it was 2015 and it is recognised that horse dentistry isn't as simple as putting a gag on a horse's mouth and just filing blindly with just feel. I still, to this day, have a lot of new clients that say, 'Oh, my horse doesn't need a vet for a dental, he doesn't need sedation.' The sedation is not because of behaviour. The sedation is part of the diagnosis and to be kind so that the horse's mouth is more relaxed to use a gag and jack it open without hurting them. Also, vets use head torches to ensure they can see any other issues in a horse's mouth.

These two horses were classic examples of why a vet is needed. Both were still acting like they had a headache or tooth pain, especially when putting pressure on their Temporomandibular joint (TMJ) or jaw point. I insisted my preferred vet who did dentals have a look at them. The first one had the very last tooth on one of the top sides of his mouth that had grown so long it was pushing into the bottom jaw. The other horse had the opposite. One bottom tooth that had grown so long it had grown up into the top jaw. If you just put a gag on these horses and stuck your arm down their mouth it would feel smooth, but that was far from what the horse was experiencing.

Once both these horses had this corrected, they needed six weeks for their jaw to recover. I then took them back and worked on some lateral work mainly and both had major turnaround in their behaviour. Both left much happier, calmer and owners ecstatic. I love my job.

During this time, we also had issues with Chika. We had taken him and Takota away camping with us overnight. There were some interesting people there and they kept visiting our horses. It made me very uncomfortable. It was in Gembrook, so not far from home but once we were there, we used the float to sleep in. Our float had bunk beds in it, so we slept on top and both my boys underneath with Mattie in swags. The horses were in yards the park provided just behind the float and I heard the people camping just down from us arguing and commotion through the night. It is hard to wake everyone and pack two horses, and kids all up in the middle of the night, so we waited till morning. Everything seemed quite normal in the morning, but we packed and went home anyway.

A week later Chika was not right. He was lethargic, mild temperature and not eating as well as normal. We asked the local vet to come, and they checked as much as they could, took bloods and let us know that afternoon that Chika must have a mild infection. We gave him two sets of antibiotics which helped a bit, but just never seemed his normal self. This pattern of going up and down continued for three months or more. We had a Ross River Virus (RRV) test done on him, but the results back then took six to eight weeks to come back. In that time, he seemed ok some days and other days very lethargic and just unwell. Everything came to a head one day when I was giving a lesson on him and I noticed a wave come over him where he got more fatigued and looked like he may collapse. He changed from fine to exhausted in a minute. I stopped the lesson immediately and rang multiple vets. Chika had been given three different sets of antibiotics by now and had three lots of bloods taken over the last three months and still no answer. He was very slowly but surely getting worse. I had picked up other infection sources on other horses over the years by what I call the 'sniff test'. I would literally spend 20 minutes with the horse looking at every part of their body and sniffing to see if I could pick up on a smell of something to find an external source. That day after a very detailed 'sniff' I noticed the mildest smell of infection coming from Chika's mouth. I washed it out and kept trying to smell it again without any success but rang both the two vets I had been liaising with to have a look in his mouth. One of the vets had done his teeth a month or two before this all began so my preference was for him to look in case a tooth had been damaged at the time. It was not so I couldn't blame him, but more to give him the opportunity to check everything was the same as when he had done his dental.

The vet had Chika sedated and in the crush for over one and half hours, giving him breaks in between. He had checked every tooth, his tongue, cheeks, everything and no luck. The manky smell was nowhere to be found. At this point, my emotions bubbled out, knowing if we didn't find something we would eventually lose Chika. Through sobbing tears running down my face, I asked the vet to stick his arm down his mouth and throat as far as it could go. This was what this amazing man was going to do next anyway. It was then that the vet said, 'I feel a dot.' It was as big or as small as a match head. The vet then asked whether I wanted him to cut into his tongue to investigate or take him to the local horse hospital. I trusted this vet more than any vet I knew, so asked him to cut. It was awkward to get to as it was very far back on his tongue where the tongue is at its thickest. He gave Chika several rests in between as he had his mouth open as far as possible and kept cutting and feeling to try to find something. After a few minutes, the vet informed me that he could see and feel a small channel and suspected something may be embedded in his tongue that we couldn't see. There was a lot of blood and it took another 30 minutes before the vet extracted a very bent needle. Once straightened, it was three inches long. The needle has been completely embedded in the deepest part of his tongue. Poor Chika! That must have been agony. He had never been weird with his mouth and had never refused the bit during this whole time he had been unwell. Once removed, the vet explained that this would have been the cause of all the issues. Bute for a couple of days and one last hit of antibiotics and should be fine as tongues heal so well. Sure enough, a few days later we had our beautiful, happy, amazing boy back. I had never used or seen these types of needles before. My only thought was that he must have picked it up from the horse yard we had him in overnight. The timing of the start of the infection matched. Talk about luck and talent of the vet being on our side to find 'a needle in a haystack or a horse'.

***

Our gorgeous friend, a client from the USA, had to travel back to Sacramento, California. Her husband had been diagnosed with cancer and they wanted to go back home. They travelled back to the States shortly after and took their beautiful horse back with them. Not long after they settled back home, she invited me to visit and hold a horsemanship clinic. What an amazing compliment to consider me to do this.

She organised a group of women for me to give a clinic to. I remember getting nervous at the last-minute, thinking, I am not good enough to be giving clinics overseas. I had given a lot of clinics now and for some reason thought people and horses would be different in another country, but they weren't. I was very proud of myself for going through with the clinic. Met some wonderful people, learnt more about how people overseas manage things.

The clinic was great fun, lots of laughs, hanging it on each other's accents and slang. Everyone said they learnt a lot, and no one got hurt. My three criteria.

My American friends had an amazing property and life; they were beautiful people. Life can be so unfair and throw some awful curve balls to people that simply don't deserve it. On this trip plus every other time I travelled to the USA I always felt their horse culture was very different to ours. Each state had a favourite breed of horse. I felt California was probably the one state that had the biggest blend of different breeds. Previous trip to Montana, most of the horses were all quarter horses. Here there was a lot of variation. The facilities for people with horses were amazing. I was so blessed to be able to travel and visit my friends. Russell looked after everything at home so I could enjoy this experience and travel by myself, which I hadn't done before. I really enjoyed the whole trip and my own company for parts. Looking back, I really do think traveling by yourself really develops you as a person.

I always learnt more about better horse management practices from every one of our trips. On my last trip to the States, I saw they were very big on putting fish in horses' water troughs to control insects. RRV was becoming more prevalent down in Victoria and, because it is mosquito-borne, we changed all our water troughs to have multiple fish in them to control the mosquito population around our property as best we could.

The following year, both Russell and I visited our friend and her husband a second time. This was an amazing time again where we were blessed to have some great times with two gorgeous people who welcomed us into their home and life. I still never knew what to say knowing her husband was now seen as terminal. I was really struggling with these beautiful people I knew getting invaded by this horrid disease. We had some amazing times sharing laughter, food, and experiences. The horses' facilities again always impressed me.

Our friend took us out to Folsom Lakes, which was one of the most amazing places I have been with a horse. At that time, you paid a small annual fee, and you could go there as often as you liked with your horses and ride. It was over 11,000 acres and as far as your eyes could see, beachfront to the lake. Where you parked your float there was a round yard, massive water trough, with fish in them for bug control, wash bay area and more. The entrance to the reservoir was like the biggest arena you could ever imagine with no walls, it was fabulous. Our friend took us there a few times with her truck and gave Russell and I two of her horses to ride. It was a magical time, friendship, and place. Thank you gorgeous lady. As Russell accompanied me on this trip, we then ventured further to spend some time in Yosemite National Park by ourselves. They had a horse trail riding centre where you could go through some amazing country. We got shown an interesting video on how to ride and the instructions were strictly no faster than a walk and stay in single file. I understand all of this for safety and have the utmost respect. Russell and I were both given Mules to ride. They were not like I imagined. They were gorgeous and some as tall as 16hh. We were told they were not the same as horses and to not mess with them just let them do their job. One person told us they were very difficult to train and quite different to working with horses. As naughty as it was, Russell and I both saw this as a bit of a challenge. We had a mini bet with each other: whoever taught one of mules to half pass first was the winner. Game on.

Now if you ever talk to Russell, he will say he won, but if you hear my version I won. To be fair we were both about the same time. These beautiful creatures were no harder to teach leg yields to than any horse I had been on and to me seemed very accommodating and clever. We had an amazing ride.

Folsom Lakes, California, with our friend

***

I had been working with Panuk on and off over the years trying to get her stronger. She would drop a hind leg at the canter when in a circle or in a straight line with no one on her. She was now a four-year-old. I was still contacting vets, chiropractors, body workers asking them what it could be. Without spending thousands of dollars to do a CT scan on her in multiple areas, no one seemed to be able to help me or interested to be perfectly blunt. I had written down a list of her behaviours and there were some traits I had seen in her brother, Giha and her mum,

Koko. Giha had the same dropping of the leg issue. Was that from his accident? She had very delicate legs and apparently slightly different hocks. Not noticeable to an untrained eye. I was worried. When I tried to start her, she just felt wrong. It was like her head and neck were too heavy for her. I felt like I had to carry her head. Me being me, put the blame and try back on myself. I continued in between to give her more and more core, and neck strengthening exercises with me on the ground while trying to ride her minimal amounts in between. I still had professionals telling me I see too much and that she just needed to work more.

I had Panuk tied up one day in one of the yards. She was settled and calm. I had been brushing her when I saw a tiny mark of something on her hind left fetlock. I chatted to her as I touched the spot. With that, she kicked me flat out in the head. I flew a metre or so and hit the cattle ramp. I lay on the ground for 20 minutes or so, too scared to get up. To be brutally honest it could have been longer. I wasn't sure if I *could* get up. I don't know if I blacked out or not, everything was blurry. After some time, I felt my head and couldn't find any blood. I looked over at Panuk and she just looked back at me as if to say, 'what happened?' This occasional explosive reaction was starting to look familiar - the same as Giha. There also seemed to be a pattern between them. The issue seemed to be when things presented on the left of them. Again, I started doing my ring around to see if anyone could piece the puzzle together. The only vet that mentioned something was a racehorse vet that was injecting her hocks to try to help. He said maybe they have got something genetic. Maybe stop looking. Nothing else was said.

I still carry a neck injury to this day from that kick. One side of the soft tissue in my neck is completely different to the other side, and I have never regained the same bend towards my left.

19

The wheels began to wobble

It was 2016. Russell and I had been to see Helen before Christmas where she didn't seem right, and we were both worried. She had back pain she couldn't get rid of and it was too painful to ride a lot of the time. For someone like Helen, who was used to riding horses and being so active, this was hard. Depressing, frustrating and downright annoying, she told us. We went to visit her in February when things were getting worse. She advised us she didn't feel right over all and was going for more tests. She seemed very down. We stayed as long as we could but with the distance and workload, kids, and our own property it was always difficult to visit.

It wasn't long after that we received the news from one of Helen's dear friends that she had a type of blood cancer. Forgive me for not having dates, or medical jargon right, everything just started to become a blur. Helen was so strong and had so much more to do. I read up on the type of cancer and typically people only survived another five years or so. I was in shock. I spoke to a mutual friend who had a medical background, and it just became too real. Shortly after that I got the news that Helen had a stroke while receiving treatment.

I went to visit her in the hospital the following week. I told myself to be brave and not cry in front of her. It just looked wrong seeing her in a hospital bed. I didn't know what to say. Helen just told me everything that had happened. She then asked me to brush her hair as it was difficult for her. I remember brushing her hair thinking, how can I help. I wanted to say I would go with her back to Anglers Rest to help look after her and the property and horses, but I couldn't. I still had our own property, horses and business. And my boys were ten and 13 years old. They needed me still and I only had them half of their lives. I felt awful that I couldn't do more. Helen had made so many amazing friends over the years and from what I could tell they were all brilliant at taking turns at helping. When I went to leave her that day from the hospital, she asked to make sure someone brought a horse to the hospital car park so she could smell and touch them. It was what she needed for hope. Some amazing people made this happen shortly after that.

As I said goodbye and walked out the door, I turned back and watched Helen watch me leave. It is a look I have now seen in too many people I have lost. When I got to the lift of the hospital to leave, I broke down crying. The trip home in the car was three hours and I don't think I stopped crying during the entire trip home.

***

It was August 2016. I was trying to bury myself in work, being grateful for our kids, while still trying to balance the property and try to believe all these gorgeous souls I knew with this hideous disease would be ok. I had another dear client, Chloe, who was a friend looking for a reliable horse. She had experienced a horse with several issues that she was lucky not to get hurt from. Chloe now had one horse I had started – Scarlett, who was brilliant – and she now wanted a reliable, 'been there, done that' type of horse. Another amazing family that looked after their horses impeccably. I thought long and hard. We needed to move one of our riding horses on, as I didn't have time to work them all. It was not a decision I thought I would make, but I offered them Chika. All the younger horses of ours needed lots more work from me and Chika was the only one I knew was 100 percent sound and reliable. I couldn't sell a horse otherwise. If I ever did sell a horse that I thought may not be 100 percent (as far as that goes with horses), I would fully explain any issues I thought existed so both the horse and new owner could manage things in the best way.

Chika did have two little quirks though. One was he was slightly grumpy about rugs around his chest; a very mild version of that base of the neck irritability but that was on both sides and exceptionally mild. With body maintenance and the right sort of work, it wasn't an issue. The other issue he had since birth was separation anxiety. To this day, I have weaned all our foals the same and none of them had this issue. When weaning our foals, I would lead them out into a paddock next to their mother and with three railings in between they could touch their mother over the rails but not feed. All foals but him were totally calm with this. Chika ran up and down the fence for three days knocking his mother's head as he passed. He was still like this now if left in a paddock by himself without another horse. To the point of panic. You could take him out by himself, ride, float, go anywhere and he wouldn't care, but if left with no other horse he was quite irrational. Interestingly, a lot of horses can be like this, as they are a herd animal and this is not a normal thing to do to them, be left alone, but he was the only one like this we owned.

I asked Chloe to take his brother Giha with him so when she took her other horse Scarlett out by herself he was never left alone. Chloe agreed to this, and I am forever grateful. I knew

Giha should never be ridden again, and it is very difficult to find them a home where you can trust the owner. Another beautiful person and family that gave our boys a great life.

One day I heard one of our vets discussing with our farrier at the time a neck malformation or abnormality they were starting to see in horses. It was quite a controversial topic. I didn't pay too much attention at the time but this one vet was starting to talk more and more about it. I started hearing about cases but really didn't understand a lot about it, to be honest.

I now started putting more time into getting our younger horses going. Bella was going brilliantly and as a restart I was loving working with her. Such a sensitive heart and soul girl. Best horse I had come across for liberty work. She was teaching me some great refinement. I was still trying to work with Panuk. I felt guilty about horses we had bred, not making it as riding horses. It was becoming a thorn in my side, and I felt my dreams were starting to be destroyed. Takota was going well with Russell but had this base of the neck soreness and was slightly more reactive than your normal horse. Nowhere near the same degree as Giha or Panuk. Oniwa or Oni was now a three-year-old. He had developed a mild lameness in his left front. This was the same as his brother Ku. We had also been doing a variation of feeding and specialised trimming of his feet to try to help. He also always led with his left front. I was starting to feel the pressure of trying to breed my dream horses with all the sacrifices of time, money, and education you put into them and besides Swassis and Chika, things weren't panning out how I had wanted.

Then the worst thing I could imagine happened. Java was sick. He was lethargic, mild fever, and totally not himself. It wasn't colic but he was agitated by something under his tail. I got the vet to come out immediately and they gave pain relief and took blood samples. They agreed it wasn't colic. Several years earlier Java had been unwell with a virus. It had hit him hard then and had taken him a few months to get over. His demeanour was like that time, but way worse. The blood results came back with no real help and the vet at the time told me it was just another virus. I wasn't convinced. He turned into a puppy, only wanting to be near me and very upset and uncomfortable if not near me. Russell was away at the time, and I was getting very worried.

Java wasn't improving and the next day seemed the same. I was calling the vet twice a day to report back and was getting told it would take time. When it comes to my horses, I can get very emotional. I was becoming a bit of a stalker to the vet, as well as constantly monitoring Java, and I kept trying to explain to her that his anus looked inflamed, similar to a mare's vulva before they give birth. It was relaxed and bigger than normal like it was spreading. He was still passing droppings, so they were still convinced it wasn't colic. By day three I was getting very anxious. He would now only lie down most of the time or cuddle me. I called the vet again and said something was not right and had to be addressed. Another vet from the clinic came out. It was now after hours as they were short staffed and had a lot of emergencies that day. He was not good. I had way too much experience of seeing horses in this condition and feared we were going to lose him.

The vet checked his blood with a Serum Amyloid A (SAA) test. This is a quick, reliable blood test vets can do to identify levels or change in inflammation and infection. The results were not good. She asked if I would take him to the closest horse hospital as it was now looking like colic. I told the vet I would not take him to hospital if there wasn't a chance for him and I wasn't going to put him through surgery. I then asked for her to do a rectal before I made the decision. She was a new vet, and she was checking with a senior vet over the phone but was not comfortable to do a rectal examination in case she perforated him. If this occurred it would end his life. I understood and appreciated her honesty and didn't want her to do anything she was uncomfortable with, as I wouldn't want her feeling responsible. I then decided if there was a chance he could just be put on a drip and flushed in hospitable I would take that chance. My biggest fear was I took him to hospital and they did invasive procedures, to then have to euthanise him in a strange place. If he was going to die, I wanted him next to his two mares with me cuddling him.

I felt if we weren't totally sure there was no hope, I had to give him a chance in hospital. The vet rang the hospital and at first, they refused to take him as he was a stallion. The young vet did an amazing job of convincing them he was fine if I was with him, so they agreed – even though they were full and had no special space spare for a stallion. The vet said, 'You wouldn't even know he was a stallion – he is asleep on his owner's shoulder.' And he was! She administered some more pain relief so he would stay upright and handle the float ride to the hospital. I rang my dear friend, Elona, who I had been in the hospital with a few months earlier with her daughter's horse who had a compaction colic who was now fine. I was so grateful she was meeting me at the hospital as I needed some moral support. I got Java out of the float and one of the vet surgeons greeted us who knew me. I had been in the hospital with several clients over the years as moral support and a sounding board for listening to options and choosing the best path of action with their horses. Now it was my turn.

First thing the surgeon did was put Java in a crush to prepare him to do an ultrasound to check what was going on. They must enter the anus to do this. As soon as he inserted the probe, the surgeon said, 'This is the problem.' Java's anus passage was perforated. I knew what that meant immediately. The surgeon looked at Elona and said, 'This is the worst case I have ever seen – why didn't you get a vet earlier?'

It had been like that for, I suspect, a couple of days. The surgeon had assumed Java was hers. We both corrected him. He then apologised and I told him I had various vets up daily for the past three days. He apologised again. He must have got a compaction and, when he passed it, it damaged his passage. The surgeon repeated he had never seen one like this before. There was nothing that could be done. Euthanasia was the only option.

I thought I was going to black out. Java had been leaning on my shoulders for hours. I wanted to take him home and have his mares next to him, but the vet said it wasn't the kindest thing to do. My poor Java was in tremendous pain.

Everything I didn't want to happen was happening. We went into the padded room. I said my goodbyes and thanked Java for everything he had taught me. For giving us so many other horses and for never hurting anyone. He was the best horse I had ever ridden, and I had always felt I had underutilised his talents when riding, as I didn't have enough time to work him as well as everything else. All that talent, beautiful nature and presence was about to be taken away from me. I just wanted my time with him again. They gave him the premedication, then moved a padded wall next to him and injected his pain away. Then, with the push of a button, the wall lowered so he was lying down. I knew he was brain dead, but I cuddled him anyway. He was my king. The father of all our progeny. He had tolerated all my blunderings and never hurt me. My soul was crushed. The saying of 'you don't know what you've got until it's gone' flooded through my aching head.

I had Java brought home the next day and buried him in his paddock under his favourite tree. My heart was broken.

I was starting to get more depressed with everything that was happening. The loss of Java had hit me hard. Having two friends with different cancers was also making me constantly uneasy. I was getting increasingly concerned about Panuk's prospects and had several people wanting to buy her as we had too many of our own riding horses I couldn't work or finish starting them all.

I continued to try to work out what I could do better with Panuk and started recognising more horses with this behaviour through clients. I had started hearing about this amazing new vet in the area. Tina was a fully qualified vet who had a special interest in spinal work with horses. She was also a qualified chiropractor and acupuncturist. I was not getting the answer from the current support network I had of other professionals, so I sought Tina out and offered her to use our property as a base for her to review horses and treat. She was amazing. Very clever lady. Brilliant balance of veterinary science, mixed with Chinese medicine, homeopathic, biomechanics and exercises. Just what we needed. I was learning an incredible amount from Tina. With our horses and clients' horses, we were seeing about eight horses on average a month, all in one day.

***

Russell and I went back to the USA together for a second time. This was now my fourth trip to the States. There was a three-day International Biomechanics Conference being held in Georgia, Atlanta, that I wanted to attend. Their focus was on how to work with horses to prevent or repair navicular disease (changes within part of the hoof) and osteoarthritis. I felt that, to help our horses and others, I needed to further educate myself on current best practices. It was being hosted by a science-based trainer who worked closely with veterinary researchers. We decided to tick off some of our bucket list items by visiting San Francisco, then going to Kentucky and doing a road trip down to Georgia for the conference.

We met up with our Californian friend again. This time we only saw her, as her husband was now not well enough to travel. The reality of this awful disease was tightening its hold on his wonderful life. Our hearts were breaking. We had a lovely ride at a trail riding place on the beach. The horses weren't looked after the best, but it was great to catch up with our dear friend and experience somewhere new. When we left her to continue our trip to Kentucky, we both broke down in tears knowing the next time we were likely to meet, her life would be very different.

Kentucky was great. Driving around looking at all the horse facilities gave us lots to think about. You could drive for some time and all the fences were painted black. Then they would all change to white. We found out later most people painted whatever colour paint was the cheapest, so that's why it was in multiple properties in the area. We also noticed that most of those big studs didn't have corners in their fencing. All the fencing had curves, which for horses was so much smarter. A lot of horses get injuries from getting jammed in corners from other horses. This eliminated that issue. We went to the second day of the Lexington Kentucky yearling sales. Fascinating to attend. We wanted to travel down to Atlanta via either Nashville or North Carolina, but every night we watched the news there were riots in the streets and people were advised to avoid the area. This was in October 2016, prior to the USA elections in November. We stuck to the most direct route down, because we were quite concerned about all the disruptions and unrest happening down south.

A few hours south of Lexington, we looked for horse-riding trails to experience the area. The one-horse trail-riding place we found advised us that her horses had lost their shoes, and she couldn't get a farrier, so they were foot-sore. She did suggest that we should hire a kayak and paddle down the river. It would take about two hours. We decided to do that and were cautious at the start, as the lady offering this service had a very dry sense of humour. She reminded us we were down south and if we saw anyone on the banks of the river and heard banjos playing, just keep paddling.

About halfway down the river on our journey we did see a man and son both in overalls fishing on the bank. They also had a rifle next to them. We felt like we were being set up, but apparently not. Boy, can we paddle quickly if we need to!

At the end of the trip, the lady that we hired the kayak from picked us up. Go figure, she wouldn't accept anything but cash, so offered to drive us somewhere to get cash. Now the jokes about being down south were getting a little too real. She then informed us not to worry ... she had been the local Sheriff for years and was now retired. We had an amazing conversation with her about lots of things. Probably the most shocking regarding horses was what happened with the horses locally every winter. People in the area couldn't afford to feed them. They would either let them out of their property for the winter and then, when they had some feed for them again, would try to find them. Or take them to the local sales and put them in any empty float or horse truck and padlock them in. People who had attended the sales to buy horses and who were often disappointed at what was there would then come out to find their horse transport vehicle already full of horses from people who couldn't afford to keep them – and they couldn't even give them away. We had only been in Lexington a few days earlier at a place where, just a few hours away, horses were traded at a premium price.

We travelled a bit further south and found another horse trail-riding establishment. They had gaited horses and the experience was very different again. The owner was also a farrier and showed us some of the weighted shoes he would put on horses to train them to high gait (lift their feet high) with their feet. It was very disturbing to me. We picked up a local magazine demonstrating these show horses and, again, I do question what us humans want sometimes at the expense of an animal.

The conference was excellent from a research perspective and did make sense to emphasise the importance of correct work for building core and muscle mass for support of joints and help avoidance of some issues. I don't think it was the full panacea for fixing significant problems to full correction, though. Time will tell. It did inspire me to get more detailed with my training and that all was not lost with our horses. It confirmed a lot of what I believed was best practice at the time for working horses. To build a strong, flexible and more resilient body for what us humans require from horses.

Russell and I were both on a brilliant high when we got back to our accommodation when my phone rang. It was a dear friend from home calling. I could tell as soon as I answered the phone something was wrong. It was Elona, our friend who had started as a client for me, and then quickly became a special friend. Her family and Russell had known each other for some time. There had been a few connections between their families from various other things and, now that I was on the scene, I had grown close to this beautiful woman and family. She had been my rock through saying goodbye to Java.

As soon as I heard her voice I asked, 'What's happened? What's wrong?' It was the answer you never want to hear: 'I have cancer.' I remember that sick feeling of dread I got for the third time in as many months. Again, it is all a bit of a blur around the medical details, I just know it wasn't good. It was breast cancer.

20

The fall begins

It was 2017. I was having some good days, but was starting to feel that constant anxiety and dread I felt like a child creeping back into my life. My dad had been in a home for a few years now as his health had been deteriorating for some time. He had dementia, plus multiple physical issues. It broke my heart to see him like this. I would visit occasionally but not nearly enough, as it upset me to see such a strong, amazing man be crippled by his body and brain.

We then got advised that his best friend Jim had passed away. When Dad came to Australia, he met Jim on the boat out from Germany. Dad and Jim had spent many years working, living, and having trips together. Us kids called him Uncle Jim. He had lived with us for a small period when we were young. He was a very tall, strong man with a wicked sense of humour. I always felt safe around and with him. When I was young, Jim had bought a property in Neerim South. I have lots of fond memories of visiting. But, like we do as we get older, I stopped visiting him, being too busy in my own world. I just felt my heart was getting stomped on again. Time. The most precious gift you can give anyone, and I hadn't given enough to him.

My sisters and I went to his funeral. It was the worst funeral I had ever been to. Jim had no family in Australia. He had experienced an amazing life. The people who had entered his life in the last ten years had arranged his funeral and it was so obvious they didn't know him. I was struck with guilt and sadness and was in too much shock to stand up and say anything. They were laughing at the fact Jim had made a concrete box and buried it with his treasures in it. It had taken them days to break into, which made me smile because I remembered Jim telling me he would make sure it was protected.

Jim had told me about this box and why he had made it the way he had; the people that were now about to obtain all his belongings had no idea. It broke my heart. The treasures in this box were photos. Lots of photos of us kids. It was too sad for me to comment. I was in a world of pain even before Jim passed and now, I was just numb. Dad wasn't well enough to go to his funeral and all of us girls agreed we were glad he didn't go. Now that I am brave enough, I will say all the things I wish I could have said to Jim before he passed, or at least at his funeral.

Thank you, Uncle Jim, for looking after me whenever I was with you. Thank you for checking for monsters under the bed and in the cupboard. Thank you for playing rabbit trap with me (a game he invented where you would try to catch the other person's finger). You were right on so many things. One of his favourite sayings was, 'Do you want a drink? You need to drink. If you don't drink you won't wee. If you don't wee, you'll die.' And, 'Do you want to eat? You need to eat. If you don't eat you won't poop. If you don't poop you'll die.' This was much funnier when I was a kid. You always made me smile, Jim. I'm sorry I didn't spend more time with you.

Note to anyone out there. Age is wonderful in hindsight. Time doesn't stand still. It goes. Spend time with the ones you care about.

***

The fall begins

I felt Russell and I needed to have a bit of fun and focus on going away more and celebrating things. Appreciate that both of us were healthy and together. I booked us in for a night in Melbourne, staying at the Langham Hotel. It is a rather luxurious hotel in Southbank in the city. Great spot. We had been given a double massage voucher from Russell's kids the previous Christmas, so we used that and pampered ourselves on our anniversary of when we started dating. It was just what we needed to forget our troubles. Some pampering and quality time. It must have been good, as Russell proposed to me that night. I was thrilled and very emotional. We called his best friend and wife a little after, because they knew the depth of what this meant to us. It filled my heart with joy.

***

I was getting some work done with Panuk but I still wasn't happy. She still had the same issues, and I still felt the pressure of getting her right. It did not look good to clients, and as a trainer that didn't compete you are very much judged by where your horses were at. My depression from everything going on was starting to get a hold of me. I was starting to lose clients as people stopped asking, 'How are you?' when your response was to start crying because you don't seem to be coping.

***

It was April 2017, Easter weekend. I was having a good day and decided to change my attitude and ignore my gut. I had just watched a few horses ride past our property and, feeling the pressure constantly with Panuk, decided I would ride her out by herself. I had done this before, but didn't ride her far and only for very short periods, as she was very nervous by herself.

I didn't have this problem with horses I worked with unless there was something wrong physically that they couldn't put their full trust in me. But what I was doing was not getting us where we should be, so time to try something else. I really felt way too much pressure and was starting to question all my own theories, gut and belief about training some horses.

I saddled Panuk and she seemed to be having a good day and was rather calm. I was surprisingly calm too. We set out off the property and up the road. Typically, I would ride the other way, but this way we had a hill sooner that I had been walking her up in hand and zig zagging her down to try to build her confidence mentally and physically. We rode to the end of the road, and she had done everything I had asked. She was a little nervous but had not put a foot wrong. We were on our way back and about to start riding down the hill back to our property when I saw two other horses out riding that were approaching. Panuk raised her head as they approached but didn't seem too pumped. I knew both the riders and had started one of their horses for them previously. They were both relaxed. Everything seemed to be fine as the two horses passed from Panuk's right side to in front of her, but then past her left eye was when things changed. In a split second Panuk snorted out loud and did a 360-degree spin. I pushed my legs down into the stirrups as hard as I could to try to stay on. She had spun to the left and I felt like I was twisted to the left but still on her, I tried to stand in my left stirrup to rebalance, but my knee wouldn't work, then within another split second she spun around again to the same side. I was thrown a few metres and landed right next to a star picket. Both the other horses had shied when Panuk snorted but had jumped about only a little. Both the other riders were still on, thank goodness.

I went to stand up and couldn't. I had no pain, I assume from the adrenalin, but my left knee was jelly. It was like there was nothing to hold it together. Panuk was now as quiet and calm as anything. It was like she had a seizure or something. She had these split seconds of absolute dramatic behaviour and then calm. It reminded me of when Ethan had seizures when he was little. He had something he couldn't control and then afterwards was exhausted. Both the other riders asked if I was alright. I can't even remember what I answered exactly. I knew there was something seriously wrong with my leg, but I think I was going into shock. I said something to the effect of I was fine and that I would get Russell to come help. I rang Russell and told him to bring the gator (small paddock ute with open sides) so I could get back. He came up the road and got me to drive the gator back while he walked Panuk home. The gator was automatic, so I only needed one leg.

I can now look back when writing this and it is obvious, I was in shock and not being logical. Remembering all this – even now – makes me feel sick at the thought of my injury. I told Russell I would be fine even though I knew my knee was totally stuffed, I just didn't want it to be. I wrapped it up with vet wrap (elastic non-stick bandage) and hobbled around the house for a bit. I took some Panadol and put my leg up on the couch thinking that would fix it (lol). I rang Nurse on Call and the first thing they said was get to hospital. 'Do you want an ambulance?' I said no and told them I would see if it settles. Big mistake right here. Russell had been doing some fencing. Once he brought Panuk back he went back out and continued. Word of advice to anyone reading this. If someone has a major fall, DO NOT leave them by themselves or believe they are ok if they cannot walk normally. A couple of hours went by, and the pain was really starting to kick in and my knee was very swollen. My leg looked very wrong. I rang Russell and told him he better get me to hospital. Again, the smarter thing to do would have been to call an ambulance.

We went to the closest public hospital where they said my knee may have major damage but it could be a while before anyone sees me. They didn't have an orthopaedic surgeon, so I would have to go to another hospital. We asked what the best way to deal with this was and were advised to pay and go to a local private hospital where they had orthopaedic surgeons. We did this. I was there for three days in a bed where no doctor saw me so they wouldn't even do an MRI without a doctor requesting it. My sons had been with their father and I needed to collect them. Things were very difficult with custody and the stress of still being in hospital and losing more days with custody was doing my head in. I lost my shit and cried trying to explain everything to a nurse. The only reason I was still functioning was that the public hospital had put a full metal leg brace on me locked to 10 degrees, and I was getting as much pain medication as I wanted. After having a complete meltdown and threatening to report the hospital for taking my $500 and no one seeing me, a doctor agreed with a nurse to get me an MRI via a phone call without even talking or seeing me. Once they had performed the MRI, I left the hospital and went home. I got Russell to pick up my kids and I felt like I just needed to keep the brace on for a while and take pain meds as no one was telling me any different.

After a couple of days, I started working again. I couldn't ride, I couldn't move or even hobble without the leg brace on full-time. My leg was like a big sausage around my knee and seemed to have no structure at all. I couldn't function without pain relief. But with pain relief, leg brace and an attitude of I have no idea what is wrong with me, I continued to give lessons with me either sitting or hobbling around. It had been a week since my accident when I received a call from a private number on my mobile. It was my normal doctor. She asked if I was in the hospital or had surgery yet. I explained everything that had happened, and she was appalled. She didn't explain everything, but she said you have major injuries that require surgery immediately for you to be able to walk again. She also explained from doing what I had done over the past week I would pay for it long term. She said you have bone on bone. You have no supporting ligaments holding your knee together. I was told I had to lie down immediately and only get up to go to the toilet or bed until surgery.

It was hard to get in with a surgeon as I was not in hospital, however she said to try one surgeon she knew that loved to work on trauma cases. I had my own business, had no insurance for income or the ability to make a worker's compensation claim, so I couldn't earn any money while like this. She said he would be sympathetic to my case.

The doctor was right. This surgeon looked at me the next day. I will never forget being in his office, looking at the plastic model of a knee, with him explaining all the damage I had while looking at my MRI. On his knee model, he seemed to just keep pulling things off it trying to show me the damage. I had heard of a knee reconstruction before but never really knew what it meant. Three ligaments needed to be fixed, plus a clean-up of everything else. I asked how quickly I could start work again and was told it would probably be 12 months before it would be fully healed and strong enough to cope. He also told me that it was more than likely I may never walk again without a limp. I explained I needed to work as soon as possible as I wasn't earning money otherwise and had two children. The surgeon explained I needed to deal with it and that if I had another accident before the leg healed there would be nothing he could do. I assume that means I could either lose my leg or it just wouldn't work. Not what you want to hear. I had the surgery the next day.

The surgeon told me he did the best he could – and that it was the worst knee injury he had seen besides car accident victims. He was confident I would make a full recovery if I followed all the instructions and took the time to heal and do the rehabilitation. He still felt that, long-term, I may limp – but in the scheme of things, this was the best outcome. The pain post-surgery was incredible. I was given four different types of pain medications, including oxycodone. I had only had this once before initially in the first hospital. Now I was taking a maximum dose of this and three other pain medications just to get through a day. I was wheelchair-bound and couldn't do anything with a full leg brace on for months.

Working with Panuk

My rehabilitation goal was to be able to bend my knee so far and straighten my leg by a certain date and, even though I was doing all the correct things, I was nowhere near where I needed to be. This was when the surgeon decided I needed a second surgery of a MUA (manipulation under anaesthetic). As I waited in the pre-operation room, that was the moment when I pulled out a notepad and pen and began to write this book.

21

Panuk

I had so many amazing people that helped me through this time. Picking up my kids to and from school, taking me to appointments. You all know who you are, and I thank you. One very amazing lady that supported me through everything was a client called Jane. I had started several of her horses and I had one on our property when my accident happened. As she worked with disabled and elderly people, she brought me all sorts of equipment to help me with daily needs. Who would think that going to the toilet could be so awkward and painful without the right support? She also insisted I continue to start her horse even though I couldn't ride. I would sit in my wheelchair and talk Jane through finishing the starting process with her own horse. This helped me to no end. I lost so much business and money that year, it was hurting. Russell was amazing the whole time and I honestly don't think I would have ever recovered so well without him.

***

It has been several months since my surgeries, and I am still visiting my surgeon on and off. I have dropped a lot of the other pain medications but am finding I am getting reliant on the oxycodone. The rules with getting it are strict but due to the intensity of my injury I was still able to get some. I would hang out for the little buzz and then I could at least walk around a bit without severe pain and at least do the horse feeds and start to feel a little normal. You would think I would be aware of the addictive situation I was putting myself under. Coming from a mother who was an addicted, prescription drug addict, suffered anxiety and depression, and was a functional alcoholic, I was always very judging of people on drugs. Whether it be recreational or overuse of prescription drugs, I was always preaching and standing on my moral tower. Well, that was getting shot down quickly. I had a close girlfriend who started as a client who had a leg removed and she had lent me one of her wheelchairs. She came to visit me and picked up on my situation straight away. She took away the last of my oxycodone and replaced it with other pain relief medication she had that was non-addictive. She said I could have as much as I wanted of that – but no more oxycodone. Thank goodness she picked up the signs. I feel I have an addictive type of personality (or genes?) and that belief is the reason that I have never tried any recreational drug besides alcohol, as I am too scared I'll like it too much. That's what real friends do. Thank you.

 I was slowly getting better and although I had begun to fall down the rabbit hole of depression, I had started working horses a lot more again and was riding again. My left knee never felt the same again, but it felt strong. I have a screw and several staples in it. One staple you can feel through the skin as it is on the inside of my knee. It gets pushed on every time I ride. I went back to my surgeon one last time and asked if he could remove it as it was irritating when I rode. He smiled and said he had seen me more than any other knee reconstruction. That he had watched me walk into his room with no limp and for that reason he wouldn't remove it. He said I had now recovered better than he thought, so if it wasn't broken, don't fix it. Fair enough.

***

We had been busy planning our wedding, which was great fun and made me forget about my other troubles. We were doing a simple country wedding on our property with very little ceremony and just celebration. It was April 2018 on a beautiful sunny day. All our friends had helped for the day – from gardening and cleaning up the place to supplying flowers and decorations. We had it catered and a friend made the most delicious handmade sweets. Other friends surprised us with a bar for serving drinks from inside a horse float. I got pampered in the morning, getting my hair done, and the friends who made the bar had a talented daughter who did her best to make my face look presentable.

We got all five of our kids involved and it was just fun, celebration and laughter all day and night. You know it's going to be a great wedding when everyone there is so supportive. I started drinking champagne by midday. Russell and I greeted guests as they rolled in, creating a brilliant, relaxed country feel. We had hay bales with linen cloth on top as seats, wine barrels and our old wooden table under a beautiful country style pergola we had built. You know you are having too much fun when the celebrant takes your champagne glass off you until after the ceremony. It was perfect, country, and magnificent. Truly a wonderful day filled with love and laughter.

***

I had been constantly still talking to vets about Panuk for years and working with her as a rehabilitation case. Tina had been reviewing her constantly and I had started riding her again. My gut was still telling me she wasn't right, but I now only rode her with other horses and was particular with what we did.

***

Russell and I had ridden in the Gembrook Time Trial before with other horses and always found it good fun. It was a course set out through trails in the bush and whoever came closest to the average time won. I had won it once before on Chika. It really is luck, but just a fun ride. It was normally about two and half hours of mainly walking, some trotting and cantering with a good 20-minute break in between. Again, trying to please others, feeling pressure of Panuk not being right and everyone telling me I see too much, I took her. She was ok at the start. We went with a few other horses in our group. The further we went the more agitated she was becoming. Horses that came up behind her were the most upsetting for her. I knew this was a mistake - never stop listening to your gut. Horses that came up from the left were far worse than those on the right of her. I got to the point several times when I said this was enough and got off her, but due to stupid pressures I normally never give in to, I kept going. Jumping back on her and riding some sections. We had now been going maybe just over an hour when she really started to get upset. We were on a wide verge off the part of the ride down next to a dirt road. She started panicking and I felt I was ready this time if she went to spin again. She was so sensitive. I can't even remember what set her off, but she just started running backwards and I couldn't stop her. She continued to run backwards until she hit a tree and then jumped forward and bucked out until I was off. I tried to hold onto her from the bridle which broke, and she got free. She only ran a couple of metres then stopped and looked at me. I wasn't hurt this time, but that was it. No more. No more ignoring my gut or trying to please others. No more listening to people that aren't listening to me because they feel I don't know enough or see too much. NO MORE! I was the one always getting hurt. I walked up to Panuk; she was calm and whatever had caused what happened was gone. I spoke to her and told her no more. No one believes us, but I know you are not right. You can't help whatever is happening. The others continued the time trial while I walked by myself back with Panuk to the floats. She didn't care the other horses were gone or about any other horses we passed. She was the most relaxed I had ever seen her. I think they understand you when you have been on such a journey, and you speak to them. We are done. I'm listening to you even though no one else is. I won't ever do that to you again.

With what I had been seeing the whole time, it was something to do with her left eye. I videoed Panuk walking past several things where she always did the same thing. I would walk her past an object and when going past on her left side she would slightly arc and shy, take her past on the right eye and she acted normal. I could do the same test 20 times and always get the same result. I did several sight-checking tests with her. Sometimes she would pass them. Sometimes she wouldn't. When I asked one of the local vets to check her eyes, he advised he could see nothing but added that maybe a specialist could see more with their equipment and knowledge. We then took Panuk to one of the best local eye specialists. I showed her the videos and she agreed something wasn't right. The vet, however, found nothing. She did offer to do a further test for free under sedation called a streak retinoscopy, which was checking for refraction. I think this meant to see if her brain-to-eye messages were right.

I was about to book this in when Tina was due for her normal visit for client's horses. I got her to look at Panuk. I told her everything that had happened since last time and what happened at the Time Trial. I showed her a video of me riding Panuk downhill where she then said, 'Oh no.' She then did a couple of tests with her to check if she had neurological issues. She did. Her brain messages were getting scrambled to her feet. Her spinal cord was compromised in some way. This neck malformation I had heard whispers about was now on the top of the suspect list. I now did a lot of research and talked to Tina about this in detail. I understood what this diagnosis would mean.

It was July 2018. Tina returned the following week with my local vet, and they did a set of radiographs. It was confirmed. Panuk had a neck malformation. Back then it was called C6/C7 neck malformation but is now known as ECVM (Equine Complex Vertebral Malformation). This is a congenital disease. The vertebrae of C6 and C7 are not properly formed with parts of bone missing. This in turn affects the stabilisation of those vertebrae. The first and second ribs can also be affected. The x-rays showed Panuk had a severe case. She was what is termed a unilateral. That is, it only affected the left side. Bilateral affected both sides. Being unilateral is considered to make the neck even more unstable. She already had changes within more than one facet joint within her neck and this had caused impingement of her spinal cord. This was all on x-ray, which is seen to be the checking mechanism for this malformation. This malformation at this time was very controversial. Reports have shown that it affects more than 40 percent of some breeds, including thoroughbreds and it is a genetic disease. You try to tell a multibillion-dollar industry to stop breeding this congenital issue.

All I could think about was how it all now made sense. Everything I had seen and felt with Panuk. Everything with her mother and siblings. I had wanted to breed the perfect horses, and I had bred the perfect malformed horses. I felt sick. Everything I had put her through. My heart was crushed. My dreams were destroyed in one fell swoop.

Life felt very unfair. I had spent my entire life trying to educate myself and earn money so I could build my dream of breeding and training perfect horses. Our stud was now the poster child for this malformation. I had one last ride of Panuk. Well, a sit and cuddle, really. I got on her bareback in the round yard walked her gently in a circle and stopped her. I then bent down, wrapped my arms around her neck and cried as I had done with other horses when my heart broke for them. I told her I was sorry for everything I had done to her. I should have listened more to her, but I had everyone telling me I was wrong. The only solace I could get from this awful situation was that she had taught me more than any horse ever had. I thanked her for teaching me and vowed to use everything she had taught me to educate and help other horses and people. Help horses by stopping them from getting worked or tortured for behaviour they couldn't help due to pain. Help people from not getting hurt and understanding the possible implications this diagnosis had.

I went and x-rayed some of our other horses and any future ones we got. Both Chika and Takota, Panuk's full brothers, also had ECVM but they were bilateral. This now made sense as to why they always struggled with pain in the base of their neck and why they were needle shy. There were so many traits and I could now see some patterns. I wrote a behaviour sheet for Tina to use with her other clients as an indicator of when to test for ECVM. My understanding is that this has assisted with diagnosing hundreds more. We never x-rayed Giha, but

I suspect that being a full brother and looking at his story, he has the malformation and is unilateral. I was certain this was all coming from Koko. It explained why she had always been difficult when her head went up for worming and other things. Everything I had been feeling about our horses being different suddenly made sense.

Looking back at clients' horses over the years where we knew something was wrong – when we just didn't know what or where to look – now became obvious. I contacted previous clients and, if they still had the horse in question, they were very obliging about getting an x-ray to finally get a clear answer. Out of the five I referred, three had the malformation. The other two didn't but had severe arthritis in facet joints that were impinging on the spinal cord. I suggested an x-ray for another client's horse that was always difficult and had gotten increasingly worse over the years. I didn't feel he had the malformation, I just felt there was something wrong in his poll area (behind his ears). Both Tina and our local vet x-rayed him. Nothing too surprising in his neck, I then explained his severe behaviour around the poll, so they then x-rayed his skull. They found over a dozen fractures on the left side of his skull.

After all those years of seeing certain behaviours, I now felt I had found a major piece of the puzzle of the horse.

22

The rabbit hole

Just a warning for this chapter, go grab your tissue box if you have at all enjoyed this book so far. The ride is about to get very messy.

Russell and I had a great opportunity to go back to the USA and stay in New York. We were lucky that we were in a situation where we could get free accommodation right in the heart of Manhattan. I never thought I would enjoy such a busy city, but we both loved it. Very different way of life than we were used to. We went off the island to visit the closest horse facilities and boy was everything pricey. You needed to be extremely financial to have horses in this part of the world.

***

Even though Oni still had this mild lameness we thought we might try to start him anyway as I have found sometimes the individual horse is better once worked. He was to be Russell's horse, so I let him do the first couple of rides. Watching him, things didn't look quite right in the front end. Russell said he could feel something different in the front also. I had a ride and, yep, both front feet felt wrong. We had our local vet, who was very talented with podiatry, come have a look and do a farrier set of x-rays. Our worst nightmare came true. Oni had severe navicular disease. He had large bony growths on his navicular bones and, unless we wanted to do a neurectomy on both front feet, he would never make it as a riding horse. I'm not a strong believer in doing neurectomies. This is where they cut the nerves to a horse's feet so they can't feel pain. These nerves do grow back eventually. It is suggested that, if you have a proven riding horse, this may be an option. Oni had struggled ever since he was a yearling. I wasn't going to do this. We did ask to x-ray his neck to check for ECVM, even though I didn't think he had it. I was right. What they did find was interesting. C4 and C5 vertebrae in his neck were slightly rotated. The vet said that, with that neck, he had no choice but to point with the left leg. Was this another type of breeding fault? I had always been told it was not genetic but a confirmation predisposition. Whenever I looked at his mum, Yella, she would always rotate her head weirdly too. His full-brother, Ku, had also been diagnosed with navicular now. With that, at the ripe old age of four-years-old, Oni was retired. My heart was sinking further every day with the bad luck we were getting.

***

At the end of 2018, Russell and I went to visit Helen and see how she was doing. She was now permanently in a wheelchair and her legs looked very swollen. She was tired and still frustrated by her disease and physical health. She asked if I wanted any of the horses, as she was trying to drop numbers. We walked the entire property and checked out all the different herds. There was a two-month-old buckskin filly. She was bold and thick-set. Friendly and chilled. Her mum was a thoroughbred/

Clydesdale-cross. I had an instant liking for her. That afternoon when we went back to talk to Helen, I said I liked her. She said I had picked the best horse on the property and that she was only ever going to go to us or one other person. The other person hadn't asked about her, so she was now in line for us to own. Once she was weaned and I had done some work with her I would come back and get her, probably at the end of spring. We talked to Helen about coming and staying with us in March when she was due to come to Melbourne to get more tests. I had arranged for Jane to come and stay with her, so she had full care. I was excited that Helen would see our place for the first time and be able to visit Bella. The reality, though? I was shocked at how much her health had declined and, once we left, I cried all the way home. Russell and I decided that, if we got the filly we would call her Packer, after Helen. Life was throwing hand grenades at everyone I loved.

***

January 2019 and we were in the car on a trip away. I was scrolling through social media when I saw a notice that our close friend's husband from America had passed away. My heart felt like it was bleeding. I texted her to give our condolences, I never know what to say to people during terrible times. Cancer had taken his life and left an amazing friend a widow. If I could have, I would have jumped on a plane to see her. I just couldn't leave my kids, and, in her grief, I don't even know if she would have wanted me there.

The following month, I had a client forward me a screenshot of a notice on social media again. This time it was informing of Helen's passing. I couldn't believe it. I rang a close mutual friend who confirmed and filled me in on all the details. No, this wasn't fair. We never got to have our last conversation. I never got to discuss everything I had come across lately with her brilliant mind. No, she was strong. We were going to spend more time together. The loss and guilt I felt was overwhelming. I spoke to Catherine, who ran Helen's property still and got the details of the memorial. Helen didn't want a traditional funeral.

Two days before the memorial both my boys got chicken pox, so I was unable to attend. I was devastated. Our mutual friend didn't go either, as the date was moved at the last moment and he felt his heart might break. He also would have struggled to get the time off and was interstate. The turnout, I heard, was amazing. Just like Helen.

I was falling back down the rabbit hole of sadness. I don't think it is fair to call it depression. It wasn't a chemical imbalance, it was an enormous amount of grief for too many losses. Please do not hang me out to dry on this - I'm no expert. I went to see my psychologist again to fill her in. I asked whether I needed to be medicated as I was so down all the time. We talked a lot about how medication works and about the sheer emotions your brain puts you through every time you encounter a death. We decided not to medicate but I visited her constantly to try to stay functional.

My work was still a little slower than I wanted. Now that I was getting labelled more as the trainer who sees things, I learnt that some people don't want to know. A lot of people do want to hear there is a real physical reason why things are happening with their horse. Of course, unfortunately, a lot would prefer to just sell them on, rather than stop the cycle of confusion and constant trainers for some horses.

Money is often the biggest factor. For a lot of people, ego is the other. If this horse can't do what I want it to do, I am not going to investigate why but palm it off to someone else and play dumb. I am not saying every horse that has something wrong needs to not be ridden. I am saying we need to support their needs to ensure that they are not excessively in pain for our needs. If their issues are excessive and cannot be fixed to the extreme, and if they are dangerous, neurological, or erratic, then the cycle should be ended. Whether that means you have them in a safe retired environment or euthanasia is a personal decision. Most horses, I have found, all have something minor just like people. They also need exercise to keep them going. It is the art of working them to benefit their wellbeing.

My girlfriend, Chris, would say that she can't believe all the horses I come across with issues and that it wasn't like this when we were teenagers. I think the biggest reason it wasn't like that back in the 80s was that, if your horse was playing up, less was known or done. If the vet said they couldn't see any obvious reason, no one investigated or sent them to a trainer, a lot of the time they just went to the market. The biggest reason personally I saw all the issues was because I was a trainer. Not a trainer that focuses on competition horses but getting the basics brilliant. The next biggest reason was that I took ownership of ensuring the person had the skills to work with the horse, re-home it if it was just a skills issue and if they didn't want the journey, or find the real issue regarding any physical issues.

The other reason I felt I wasn't as busy in my work was because people just didn't want to hear about all the deaths I was experiencing. It was becoming one of the most difficult times in my life. I was starting to see that those who had experienced similar were very supportive, but a lot of people just don't know how to deal with death or how to support someone who is experiencing a lot. I got told third hand I was too negative. I don't understand people sometimes. Horses are easy, people not so much.

As I now didn't have a riding horse, I started looking for one. A girlfriend found a nice two-year-old gelding that I went and saw. Now another lesson to be learnt. I am great with being very objective with horses, checking them out for other people. For me, I get sucked in with personality. This bay was gorgeous, Friesian crossed with riding pony and thoroughbred. He was unstarted and untrusting. Perfect! *Hmmmm…*

I worked with him a little at liberty while at the owner's property. I could see there was a lameness issue, but his feet were so rank that could have been the cause. It is hard to pick if there is something else going on if a horse is sore in their feet. He was very smart. I had worked with him for ten minutes or so and then you could see the penny drop. He walked confidently into me and dropped his head into my chest. I really liked this horse. Then, just as we were having our moment a wedge-tailed eagle flew extremely low over our heads. I looked at the owner and said, sold.

To me, it was a sign from Java. Every time I rode Java out at home, we had wedge-tailed eagles follow us. I bought a lot of things on emotion. Considering what had been going on, not surprising, I suppose … The owner of the horse said she had never seen a wedge-tailed eagle there ever before.

✳✳✳

I had been avoiding dealing with Panuk and had convinced myself she would be fine retired in the paddock, so I had put her back in with Koko, her mother. I was starting to notice the progression of her neck was increasing. If Panuk turned her neck a certain way sometimes, it was obvious there was pain. She didn't spin or run backwards anymore. Instead, she would stand perfectly still, as if she was too scared to move. I watched her sometimes when she would eat her hard feed and, if she suddenly looked to the left and she felt the pain or pinch, she would stop eating and stand still like a statue with real fear in her eyes. It then progressed further, so that she would sometimes stand in the paddock by herself and, when the other mares moved too far away, she would neigh for them to come to her. They would just look back at her as if to say there is no fence in between us, just walk over. But she would stand sometimes for hours – perfectly still and alone – limiting her movement so she wouldn't feel the electric shock go through her body each time when her spinal cord was being pinched. When I saw this happen three times in one week, I decided to euthanise her.

I called Tina and begged her to dissect my beautiful horse so others could learn from her. She asked me to wait a little longer as she was busy. I understood, but I told her I was going ahead with it anyway, as it was now cruel to keep her in her world of terror. I organised a vet who was a friend to come and perform the euthanasia. The next day, Tina called back to say she would come to do a paddock dissection by herself. This is extremely difficult, as it is very physical and time-consuming for just one person. I was eternally grateful.

The day came for us to say goodbye to Panuk. It was winter and it was mild but raining consistently. Both vets who came were people I consider friends – and some of the most thoughtful people I know. Peter, who knew Panuk and I well, understood from what I had explained to him that when her head went up everything was more of an issue. We fed her handfuls of lucerne hay in the rain, opposite her mum, so she was as relaxed and comfortable as could be.

Peter gave her the first sedative intravenously and, as it hit, I took the lucerne hay away. I told Panuk, like I had told so many horses before her, how much she meant to us. I thanked her for teaching me and apologised for not picking things up sooner. I hoped she understood how lucky I felt I could kindly end her pain. Peter was amazing with how gentle and caring he was with both of us. As soon as Panuk was gone, Tina stepped in and asked me to leave the property for the day. I had arranged for a digger to come in and bury Panuk and had given Tina his contact details so Panuk could be buried before I got home.

I was inside, getting my things together to leave. I should have been more organised, but I was so confused in my misery. As I was about to leave the house, I heard an enormous thud. I can only assume that had been Tina lifting Panuk's head and neck into the back of her car. I felt sick. I went straight to my car, grabbed Matilda our dog and left. I can't even remember where I went or what I did. I just remember the phone call about five hours later from Tina. She told me it was the worst case she had seen and explained the biomechanics of what the missing bone was like in her neck and how, on the left side, the bottom two vertebrae of her neck had nothing to support them. Her ribs were not affected though. I was in a daze. I had just begged someone to chop up my baby who I had been asking vets for seven years what was wrong. My science head was battling with my mumma bear instincts for my horses. What the hell had I done?

A couple of weeks later, I decided to get a definitive answer on where the genetics had come from. I didn't want to exhume Java's grave and so I booked Koko in to have her neck x-rayed. I was walking a horse down through the paddock towards the arena to work when I saw Koko. I knew instantly something was wrong. She looked like she had colic. She was just standing with a drooped head and a painful face. I put my client's horse away and ran back to grab Koko. I could tell instantly she was in a lot of pain. She was also lame. We had experienced a lot of rain, and all the paddocks had a fair bit of mud in the lower parts. Koko was black and as it was mid-winter, had a long fluffy coat.

She had fresh mud sprayed up her legs, so I couldn't see any issues. I had given her and Yella some hay that morning and had watched them both canter up and munch on their hay. I couldn't work out how things could have changed that quickly. Once I got her out of the paddock, I hosed down her legs and noticed a small clean-looking puncture wound on her fetlock. The entry point was tiny, but I knew from experience it was in the worst spot possible to have accessed her joint capsule. I checked her temperature and it was elevated. I called the local vet immediately. I knew too well what this probably meant. Best case scenario: lameness not from puncture wound, and her temperature was caused from a mild virus. That way, I wasn't going to have to deal with a horrible decision. Who was I kidding? If it looks like an elephant, smells like an elephant and acts like an elephant, it is an elephant. Joint infection and, this far along, because she had a temperature, her chance of survival – even with possible surgery or just antibiotics – was low.

Once the vet arrived, pain relief was given immediately. This barely made a difference. The vet put the joint under pressure to check if it was compromised and couldn't get the full response as Koko was still in too much pain. It was obvious though that was the issue. She was given a less than 10 percent survival rate and, with other issues she had increasing over the last few years, we decided to euthanise her. I was in shock, again.

The digger to bury her was hours away. I couldn't stand being outside, so I hid inside until I calmed down. A few hours later, I realised our dog, Matilda, was missing. Could things get any worse? Oh yes, they could. I had chosen to euthanise Koko via lethal injection and, once she passed, everything relaxed under her tail. Let's just say it looked a little bit too much like a steak. Matilda had been having a snack and ate part of Koko. I was mortified and had to rush Matilda to the vet. The drugs hit her within the hour, and she had trouble walking. They decided to put her on an IV drip to help flush her system. In one day, I had lost my main broodmare and now possibly our dog, due to my carelessness. At this stage, I was pretty much a gibbering mess at the vet hospital. Matilda survived. I was grateful for that. Our beautiful kelpie meant the world to us.

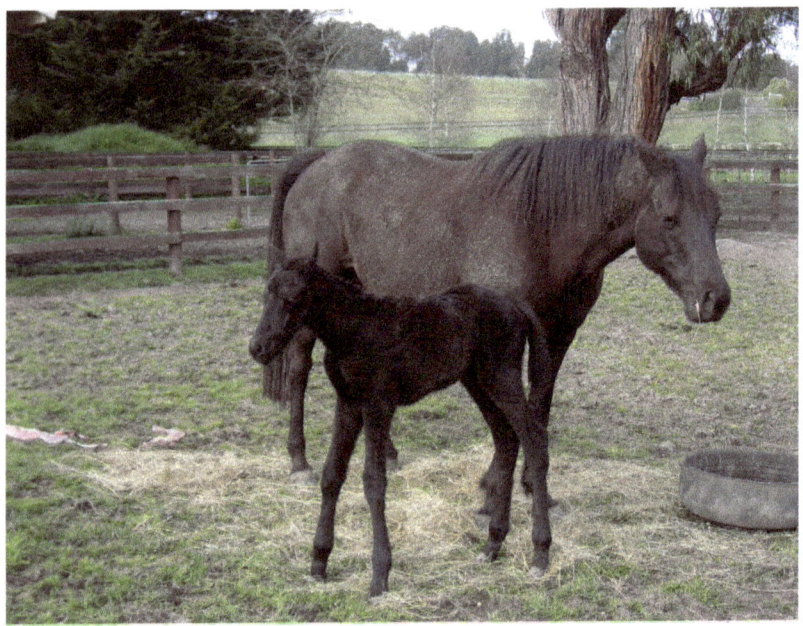

Koko when she had Panuk

The following week, my dad passed away. With everything going on in my life, I hadn't visited Dad nearly enough. He had been in a great nursing home now for years. The staff were amazing and had built a lot of rapport with him. He hadn't known who we were for a few years due to his dementia. I could write a whole other book on the details and memories of my dad, but it is still too painful to talk a lot about. We were lucky enough to spend some time with him before he passed. Just like all the horses I had said goodbye to, I was blessed to cuddle Dad while he was unconscious and thank him for always being there for me and for everything he did. I think my dad was amazing. He had been a grumpy, opinionated man a lot of his life, but he was heart and soul. And he was my dad. He had brilliant ethics, a naughty sense of humour and I loved him. When I think about the conditions he grew up in and the circumstances he endured, I do think he was brilliant.

We had a lovely, relaxed memorial at a pub, just to piss him off. He always told us not to have a funeral; it was a waste of money. We used to say back to him, 'Ok, but we will have a party – it's about us surviving without you.' He would always laugh at that. This gorgeous man gave his body to science. So many medical students sent us thank you letters once his ashes were returned after two years. This is where I got this trait from.

A month after this, I attended a three-day horse dissection. It was July 2019. Tina often assisted the researcher who performed these dissections. Amazing learning opportunity. Tina had asked my permission to bring Panuk's neck out at the dissection as a learning opportunity. I was fine with this. I found the dissection an even more brilliant learning opportunity than I had imagined. It confirmed so many things I had been teaching clients and myself about how to work with your horse to support their body. The researcher was so skilled and had a wealth of knowledge. Back in my corporate days, I had an assessment done and it showed I was over 90 percent visual for learning. Watching every part of the horse, the layers and mechanics just clarified things I visualised happening beneath the skin.

I was then asked if I would talk to the group about Panuk. Her story. I explained I would love to, but that everyone would have to excuse my tears. It helped a little with the healing process. I hadn't seen Panuk's bones before and Tina brought them out for me to see before I talked. They had also preserved the bones of her skull. I didn't know that was happening, but I was grateful. It showed how her whole jaw was slightly tilted which was a direct correlation to her neck. The researcher informed us that her USA team had confirmed the same data, that ECVM could now be picked up with a jaw x-ray. It also answered why from birth, Panuk had an abnormal tooth on a weird angle. Peter also attended the dissection for a period which I was grateful for. I felt Panuk was being honoured. With two amazingly talented and educating vets. Tina has now written Panuk up in several papers and owns her neck bones which have educated many. Peter owns her skull and jaw bones. It gives me some peace that the two vets who were with Panuk when she passed now continue to educate others using pieces of her.

***

It was now November 2019. I was still in somewhat of a haze when we suddenly lost Matilda, our beautiful kelpie. I had noticed she had been changing, eating weird things and very low. With everything we had been going through I just assumed my depression was impacting her. We lost her within days to a rare type of blood cancer. It was normally set off by a toxic event. She had experienced a few of those in her life. At the young age of seven years old we said goodbye. Russell and I were devastated. This was my ninth death within the last two years. I attended a session with my psychologist who, when I updated her, burst out crying. You know things are bad when your mental health support person can't deal with sadness in your life anymore.

My confidence in myself, my life, was coming to an all-time low. I am not going to lie; I did consider ending my pain with suicide as what I believed might be a way of stopping the torture I felt from losing so many souls. I seriously thought about it. But I could never do it. I could never put the people I love through that. My sons, husband and step-kids mean everything to me. That is only inflicting on others what I was feeling. It was never going to be a real option. *If anyone does read this book and has felt like this, please talk to people. Even a stranger. Get professional help. Suicide is not the answer. I have experienced amazing joy since this time. I also enjoy moments in life greater than I ever had before. I understand things can change in a blink, so tell those around you what they mean to you. Smell the proverbial roses.*

23

Rebuilding my happiness

I felt I had to rebuild my happiness. Packer was now weaned and almost 13 months old. I took Swassis with me back to the High Country to help me bring our new baby home. I had my close friend go with me as well. Elona was now in remission from her breast cancer and was up for the road trip. Russell and I had gone up a couple of months earlier to halter break Packer and get some basics done with her to help for the trip home. Elona and I spent five days there, working with Packer each day and getting her to bond with Swassis for the float trip home. The trip from Helen's was about 45 minutes of tight, winding roads with sheer drops on one side. The type of roads that, if a horse went off in your float and caused it to move, you may not make it out. The rest of the trip was slow going with a float … almost six hours.

I worked with Packer for a few days, getting her comfortable with leading, being confined in the float and tied up. I was feeling positive. I'm not the type to just shove them in the float and drive and see what you have at the end. I have had to retrain and deal with way too many horses with floating issues to go down that path. I have also seen a horse go through the roof of a float, the back and even try to jump out through the front window. It makes me laugh when people find it hard to get horses on floats. That's not the real issue. The issue is them being comfortable and confident in the float. In the nicest way, Packer was going too well. I felt I had to push her a little harder so I could deal with her rebellion outside the float, rather than her possibly losing her shit in the float on the way out. I had brought some sedation to help for the first part of the trip but knew from experience not only can a horse break out of sedation, but you need to have your horse relaxed going in and staying in the float for it to be a complete success.

The second last morning before we left, I could see Packer was getting a bit over it and so I took the opportunity to push her a little. She needed to stay calm and in a float for possibly up to seven hours tomorrow, I needed to ensure she could cope. As expected, once I continued to push, she came out fighting like someone trying to say they have had enough and that no one was listening. She started to pull back and rear with twists. This is normal behaviour and, although I don't like doing it, it is part of working with horses. It was all going well until Packer pulled further and further back towards a shed. One leg went down next to the edge of the shed where there was an exposed edge of the tin. I got her out and she was unharmed, which was attributed to luck more than my management. The next time I asked her forward, she responded softly with a try. I put her away till the afternoon to allow her some more thinking time. I then brought her and Swassis out. Packer loaded as kindly as Swassis and both relaxed and munched on their hay with the float all closed. There was no fear or lack of understanding. She had learnt to yield softly to my requests and the float had become her haven.

I was feeling confident for the next morning when we had planned to leave. My anxiety the night before was due to my own demons questioning if I had done everything the best I could to prepare Packer for the trip home. I had probably now worked with a couple hundred horses floating and my brain told me it was all good, but my heart was telling me she was precious cargo.

The morning we were set to go, the horses seemed pumped more than they had been. The mob of kangaroos that were always surrounding on the paddocks were closer than they had been. As I was leading Packer out of the yards and past the cattle ramp, a kangaroo flew past, which caused her to jump and try to bolt. She ran backwards into the cattle ramp and smashed one of the railings. She was now even more pumped. I had been thinking of not using the sedation to float home as she was so chilled in the float. Not worth the risk. I waited for her to chill a bit outside the float and then gave her the oral sedation. After half an hour or so she was ready for a nice rock in the float. The sedation worked perfectly. She didn't move a step and by the time she was well out of sedation she was happy and relaxed in the float travelling. We stopped every couple of hours to give hay and offer a drink. Although I never travel horses for more than three hours straight without a break and walk them off the float to get their head down, we didn't risk it with such a young horse that had never seen anything but the hills of the high country. We got Packer home safe and sound. She was beautiful.

***

Although both Russell and I were still mourning losing our dog, Matilda, we both had trouble sleeping and feeling relaxed without a dog. It was March 2020. I had been searching for a kelpie puppy when one caught my eye. There was a photo of three very serious red kelpies all sitting properly with one black one photobombing. The black one was a girl. She looked exactly like her brothers but was black with very slight tan points. We thought maybe she wasn't purebred, but it didn't matter, she had our hearts. The property she came from was a dairy farm. The house had no glass in the windows and the puppies just bounced everywhere. When we got her home, we tried to implement the same rules Matilda had followed … not a chance. We learnt we had to customise her training to suit her and her personality. This was Abbey. She was different to Matilda, which is what we needed. No dog could replace her, but Abbey could help us heal. We soon learnt she could also teach us to laugh again. As she had had no glass in her previous home, when she first wanted to go outside of our house she just purely ran flat out at the windows. She hit them with a thud, shook it off, then tried again. Besides thinking we had just bought a brain-damaged puppy, we laughed and laughed. She was also super affectionate and clingy. Normally not what we were used to, but what we needed. Abbey grew into a tall dog with long hair on her tail. We worked out that she is what is called a Barb kelpie. Named after a gentleman's wife, Barbara, from the 1890s who crossed a collie over a kelpie to get a taller, friendlier dog to interact with the animals they were working with. This was Abbey to a T. She would lie for hours playing with our two steers. Licking their noses, pressing her head against theirs. She brought back a lot of joy into our lives.

24

The world stood still

Around the same time we got Abbey, we looked for another riding horse for Russell. Now that we understood what some of our horses had, we no longer pushed for answers. The joys of ECVM were the multiple lameness and neurological issues that followed with some. It was very dependent on the degree of the malformation, the age of the horse, and what work had been done with them. Also, what injuries etc had occurred in their life. Takota was now showing several issues and so was retired at ten. Such a waste of a beautiful horse. I hated being in the market for horses, as what some people consider normal always amazes me. I find the majority of people feel it is acceptable that a horse is systemically tight and sore. The level of care is so varied and unfortunately people lie to make or save money. However, there are a lot of good horses out there and some great people that do the right thing and are honest. You just need to find them. Horses are very stoic. I am constantly amazed at what a horse will tolerate and yet how easily you can lose one.

***

We all started hearing about this virus. My oldest son was interested in medicine and was keeping up to date with all the latest. Stupid us, we were making fun of him when he started wearing a mask in public. Two months later was lock down and compulsory mask-wearing. Living in Victoria and having the most severe rules and restrictions of any city in the world had its implications on so many levels. Covid. Who would have ever believed that people would have been stopped from going to work? That you could lock entire cities down. Most people had never experienced this before in their lifetime. Like a lot of others, I had to stop work and initially, I felt like this was a forced holiday of sorts. Both my boys were still at school. One in year twelve, the other in year nine. I felt like they were missing out on so much but to put it in perspective, they were healthy and fine. I will not go into my thoughts on this, as I found this was quite a touchy subject for many. I do think it was a good reminder to people of what is important in life.

Like a lot of others, I probably started drinking too much alcohol and started getting into bad habits. I am forever aware of my family history, and this is probably the main reason over the years I learnt to rein back on alcohol use. I have seen way too many times, the devastation it causes to the individual and the people around them. It was August 2020 and we were in one of our strictest lockdowns when I saw on Facebook that a work acquaintance, who I viewed more as a friend, had passed. Linda lived in another state, and I hadn't talked to her for a few weeks, but I had read her posts through her business page and personal page the day before and I felt in my mind that something was going on. I had no idea what. Linda was a kind, generous and considerate person and always posted lots of thought-provoking sayings, poems, and quotes. I read through all the comments to try to work out what had happened when in the back of my mind I feared the worst. I had seen, several years earlier at a clinic, a look in her eyes. I have seen this look too many times when someone wants to say goodbye but doesn't know how to. We had talked so many times since the clinic. Linda was always so friendly, honest, and great to talk to. We had chatted a lot about our lives as we had both experienced a few similar things. The last time I spoke with her she seemed very happy, and had a great family, husband and more.

The more I read the more it sounded like she chose to leave. The funeral was via Zoom as I wasn't allowed to travel due to Covid restrictions and funerals were restricted interstate to direct family members. My mobile wouldn't work so I had to use my youngest son's mobile to watch the funeral. It was one of the saddest things I have done. Linda had committed suicide. They didn't hide the fact and asked everyone to talk to others if ever feeling this way. My heart plummeted for her husband, family, and friends. I could but couldn't comprehend how such a beautiful woman could choose to leave this planet. She was an amazing person. This brought up lots of issues for me as it does for everyone. I just felt so useless. I obviously didn't know her that well even though we had had some lovely heartfelt discussions. I just didn't know what to say or do. Linda, if you are reading this, I hope you are in a happy, peaceful place – riding free.

Covid had now come to another level for me. I just wanted everyone out again. We had now lost ten souls in the last two and half years. Death was coming into our life way too often.

***

It was now November 2020. I had my beautiful puppy, saw lots more of my boys and I was learning more and more to enjoy the moments. Relish in the times when things were good. Work had picked up even with lockdowns as people were getting into dangerous situations with horses, so training was now an essential service for safety. It was just an average day and I had just gone to feed our horses and saw a tiny split on the edge of Packer's eye. There was a dot of blood, but only a minor cut so nothing to worry about.

A month later, I noticed a wart-like growth in the same spot. I thought straight away it could be a sarcoid (non-malignant skin cancer), so treated it the same way I had now treated lots of others successfully. Instead of shrinking the growth, it was causing it to double in size daily. The vet came and had a look and sent photos off to a specialist surgeon who confirmed my fears that it looked like the most aggressive type of sarcoid you could get, and immediate surgery was the best option. Within a few days, we had Packer at Ballarat horse hospital having surgery. She was only two years old. The wait during the surgery was horrific. The surgeon said one eye would look smaller but was hopeful to remove a big enough margin to not affect the actual eye but rather just the surrounding tissue.

After three hours, we got the phone call from the surgeon saying he felt he did the best he could have. It was very aggressive and the tumour was four times bigger under the skin than above. Even though we acted quickly, if we had left it much longer they would have had to remove the eye in order to have any chance of her surviving. The surgeon inserted chemotherapy beads into the remaining tissue to address any possible rogue cells. Packer had behaved perfectly, and they told us how much of a gem she was for such a young horse. Within weeks two small tumours started coming back. I was panicking. The surgeon had explained this could happen and we then needed to hit them hard with a drug called Equi Immune. My understanding is that this is a live bacterium that targets abnormal cells. The injections were done straight into those areas. Her eyelids blew up like she had been hit with a baseball bat. Packer had this done three times over a couple of months. If this didn't work the only choice would have been to go back into surgery and take a bigger margin including her eye. I was not willing to do this.

Her eyelids continued to be swollen every time she got more injections. Then one day I saw two perfect holes in her flesh where the tumours had started coming back. If I pushed around these holes where her eyelids were still swollen, she had thick yellow puss come out. My vet and surgeon were very excited and had a discussion saying this was the best thing that could be happening. I then promised myself that if Packer lived, I would sit on her for her third birthday. For the next month I saline washed the two holes around Packer's eye and squeezed out close to half a cup of pus every day. It finally started to dry up and eventually heal.

***

It was now January 2021. We finally found another riding horse for Russell. We came across a beautiful six-year-old gelding, Prophet. He was a 16hh Friesian/Cob-cross and he picked Russell to take him home. Prophet had a few issues and acted pretty much like a 600-kilo baby sometimes, but Russell adored him and worked well with him.

On Packer's third birthday, I worked with her a little in the round yard. I then got on her and had a sit for the first time. Like most horses I started, she was relaxed and almost asleep. I wasn't planning on starting her then, she was too young. I just needed to feel full body contact for everything we had been through and what she meant to me. I wrapped my arms around her neck and cuddled her while I sat up on her. It had been almost a year since our cancer fright and she was still with me. I relished the fact I was doing this on her. Instead of being the final time when I had to say goodbye on so many others. When I got off her, I walked to the edge of the round yard, then sat down and cried. Packer walked straight over and dropped her head in my hand with her smaller eye pressed in my hand. She just left it in my hand for what seemed like a long time. The world stopped turning in that minute for me. It was the ultimate way of thanking me, I felt. It was just us in the world. Who says horses don't know? I knew then Packer was an old soul and we had found each other. Through all the pain of all the deaths, injuries and heartache, this girl could melt my soul and make me feel like everything was ok and life was good.

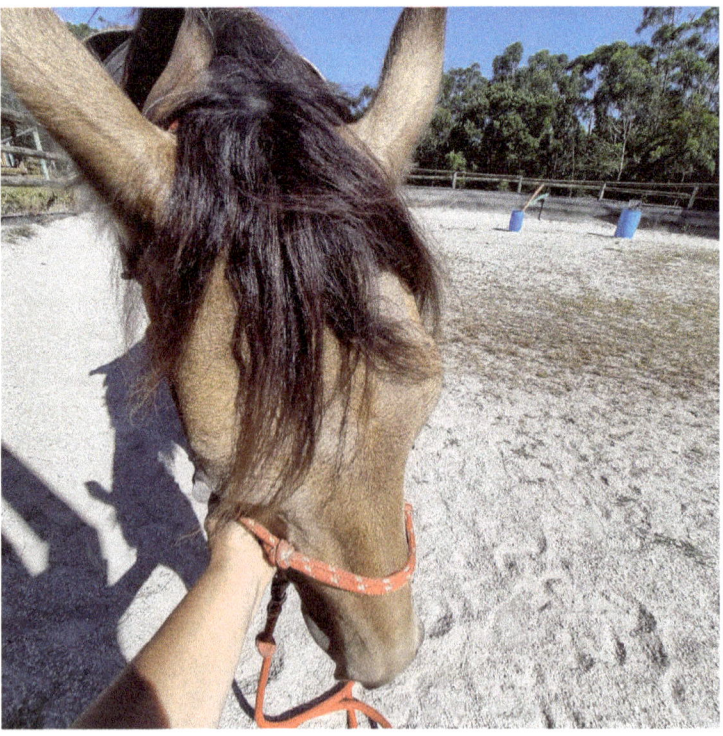

Packer placing her recovering eye in my hand

25

What have I learnt?

Through all my experiences, life, and work with horses, what have I learnt? Now that could be another book. In a nutshell. What to look for with horses when things are going well, and/or when things are not. I have had some great performing horses in my life, but it is the constant problem horses I had thrown at me that really taught me. Breeding-malformed horses has taught me how to see the signs from an early age. Living and working with so many horses has given me a pattern of things to watch for. Although for a long time I played the victim of poor me, why do I have so much bad luck with our horses, injuries, breeding issues and other health problems. I now see it as every horse has taught me something. It is all these gifts of something that have assisted in my mind knowing what it does. If that has assisted or saved one person or horse from unnecessary trauma and an understanding so both horse and owner experience less pain, it was all worth it.

If money wasn't an issue, I would love to set up a horse centre. One on a bigger scale of what we currently do. Instead of getting other consultants in, they would already be here. When a horse arrives, all physical checks and behavioural assessments are made. We then, as a combined team all in one spot, work through all the issues to then come to the best solution for owners and horses. Put them on a training path. Work with horses and owners in rehabilitation for their specific case. Retire the horse if necessary for pain, danger management or euthanise cases where that is the kindest outcome, rather than put the horse back out into the public.

I often feel people look short-term for instant gratification. I often say I don't think many people on the planet wouldn't bend their ethics for sex, drugs or money. This short-term thinking doesn't work with horses, or people.

Enjoy the moments that make your heart sing. Make you feel safe and loved. Find that thing that makes you happy, gives you peace, feels like home, and is meant to be. That you can lean on in hard times. Whether it is a horse, dog, walking, sport, crosswords, or craft. Doesn't matter; have something healthy for your mind. Spend time with the people that matter. Time and your heart are the biggest gift anyone can offer. Don't waste time with those around you who are toxic or just don't get you. Yes, we are always on a constant improvement journey, but if you are always told how you think or feel is wrong, find the type of people that get you and think you are amazing.

Don't torture yourself about bringing up kids, work, or a partner. Remember balance. Be strong and do your best. If you can look in the mirror and see past the wrinkles to a kind and considerate soul, you have done amazing.

Bloody hell, I'm starting to sound like some sort of Yoda. These are just my learnings, in my life so far. Everyone has a story, find the time to listen to them. I still stuff up. I still wish I did better, but I cut myself some slack now. I still learn things every day in my job working with horses. I am blessed to have a great network of professionals around to always advise me.

Eight years after my accident, looking back at the questions I asked myself as I was going under a general for my second surgery has given me the time and space to be sure of my answers.

Why am I here?

Because I was trying my best to work out what was wrong with Panuk and help her.

What did I do wrong?

Nothing. I consulted with other professionals and weren't getting the answer. Things happened, so I finally got my answers.

What did I miss?

Nothing. Trust your gut. I, plus the whole horse industry, just need to continue to learn that this malformation can have major behavioural impacts, especially when impinging on a spinal cord in multiple places.

Could this have been avoided?

Yes, but if I hadn't continued I may have never found the answers I now know.

Had I done the work I needed?

Yes, plus more.

Maybe if our relationship was better?

Looking back, we had a brilliant relationship. Panuk couldn't help her reaction to her spinal cord being twisted. She was a sweetheart and taught me and others so much.

Will I ever work again doing what I love?

I have already been and, through what I have learnt, hopefully, helped several others. I know that within my clients, over the last eight years, I have picked up several other unilateral horses with ECVM that were dangerous, and if the person listened, they were now safe. For those who didn't, several have been hurt.

Have I lost my credibility?

Nope. For the people who listen and want the truth regardless of how difficult, no. For those who don't want to hear as they want to pretend everything is ok, not spend the money or sell their problem on, yes. I lost a few clients. I often got told it was because I saw too much. The ones that think this is a problem I lost. Those who embrace it and want to work with their horse for the best physical and mental relationship we are powering. Horses are incredible and to ignore their pain and believe it is all just bad behaviour I feel is ignorance. Everyone has their journey and there are many other amazing people out there to help.

Am I being selfish to my boys?

No. I have done my best and taught them about passion, ethics, and beliefs. How to make a change, even if only in a small way. I have tried to be a good example. Life doesn't always go the way you want. Find something that makes you happy and channel that when things are not so good. Lean on the people who care the most about you.

Is this going to be used against me by one or two people who have been incredibly unkind to me?

Yes and no. I feel I have scared some people off. My clients often laugh when I go to check out horses for them to purchase and say 'yes'. I will still refer them to a vet check for big-ticket items, but for behaviour from lack of training versus pain, I can see and feel a fair bit. I often say that if I were to personally go get a vet check I would fail. I limp when I get up in the morning, but then I am fine and, most of the time, feel better the more I work and do. Horses are the same most of the time. The right sort of work helps and improves their body and mind, so they are happy, pain-free riding horses. However, there are some I see as having familiar traits or behaviours that are red flags – and in those cases, I would walk away unless you want the journey of spending a lot of money, getting injured and the heartbreak of not being able to fix the problem.

Red flags – from what I have experienced and seen – include:

- A horse that cannot graze with one foot in front of the other, on both sides, reasonably equally.
- A horse that sleeps with its head pressed under the chin.
- Head pressing of any kind.
- Horses that go off like a cracker when their head goes up.
- Needle-shy horses, even after having someone really good work with them for it.

Also, pay attention to weight distribution when a horse wees. (Vets hate this one.)

These are hardly clinically proven tips, just an experienced lady's thoughts.

Red flags with people and relationships:

- Toxic people.
- People that never give back.
- Those that are not heart and soul.
- Those that are full of shit.

26

Where are things now?

Packer is now my main riding horse. I love her to bits. She is six years old, but I can ride her anywhere with anyone and we get each other. Her hocks are a bit dodgy, and she will never be an Olympic show jumper (me neither), but I trust her with my life for riding and working with other horses. She is getting better and stronger as the years go by. I can canter by myself with her through the bush with no one else around and just smile and thank Helen for the gift.

Swassis has cushings and is retired. Takota is Swassis' paddock mate and the both of them are living their best life. Bella is still going well, although now she is 15 and a few issues are showing up. Pretty much like all of us as we age.

Oniwa never came good from severe navicular and rotation of two vertebrae in his neck and we recently euthanised him. The only solace in his passing was that we stopped the pain. Looking at his family tree, and the history of his mum and brother both having neck issues, as well as both the progeny having severe navicular, it makes sense. I do think the relationship between neck vertebrae rotation and the effect on front feet with navicular, if not already investigated, should be.

I still give lessons and some clinics. We offer accommodation in our cottage on our property, with views of all our horses and others that are here. People can bring their horses and stay in comfort and learn as much as they want or just have a weekend away. I don't start or retrain many horses anymore but am moving more into an educational-style role. I check pleasure horses out for people and offer specific coaching and education customised to people and their horses' needs. I still visit Helen's and try to do some work with horses that are left, to ensure they find the best possible home. Every time I canter on Packer through the bush, I still hear Helen giggling and screaming, 'Two crazy ladies riding through the bush,' and I smile.

***

The decision to put Panuk down was not easy, and I was constantly tormented. I knew logically there was proof of her malformation and the secondaries of arthritis in four joints in her neck that caused her spinal cord to be crushed intermittently when her neck turned a certain way, but she was my baby. We bred her. Her name says it all. Panuk means, in one of the Native American dialects, 'better'. Is she a key to more people acknowledging this condition and choosing not to breed any horse confirmed with this malformation? This is easy to avoid. A simple x-ray can give the all-clear. But will the horse industry take this on board? Time will tell.

Since starting to write this book, things have progressed with ECVM, especially overseas. There are a lot of amazing, talented people working on this from a worldwide perspective. Knowledge is power. From my experience, bilateral horses can be worked and building surrounding muscles for support can only help these horses. They are still disadvantaged, compared to those without the condition. Common sense would say if you are missing pieces of bone in your neck therefore the soft tissue connection to bone and anatomy is also changed, you don't have the same advantage as those with full vertebrae. Unilateral horses, such as the ones I've experienced, I hope for those affected that there is some hope. For the ones I experienced, euthanasia was the kindest thing for all involved. Keep in mind that I have been told Panuk is one of the most severe cases my vet had seen because of the amount of bone missing.

Please understand that, as a trainer, I only get to see when things are not going so well. This disease was first seen in one breed of cattle and was bred out within several years, as the calves wouldn't live past one day-old. The horse industry is well past that now with more than 45 per cent of some breeds having this. The purpose of this book was not to throw a hand grenade at the horse industry but to highlight that horses don't lie. As humans, we are blessed that the nature of horses allows us to do what we do with them. In return, we need to show empathy and understanding to ensure we have the correct knowledge to best assist them and ensure we minimise the risk of injury to not only them but all the humans who work, play, and enjoy our wonderful horses.

My current understanding is that the horse industry is saying, literally, 'the horse has bolted' and that selective breeding to remove this is no longer an option. I disagree. I do agree there are varying degrees of this malformation, and each case can be different, however, genetically if you have it, you can pass it on. One of the biggest issues I feel is that, when a mare goes lame, rather than full investigation, the owner will (a lot of the time) breed her to have a foal to give her purpose. This is one reason why this malformation is increasing, in my view. Koko, our main broodmare, was a classic example for this. ECVM was not even talked about when I bought her, but I got her as a perfectly bred ASH that had an accident as a yearling, and her tendon made her not sound enough to ride. Why did she have the accident? All her progeny have the malformation, throwing both bilateral and unilateral. The only foal I didn't check was Giha, who had a horrific accident when he was a foal. I can almost guarantee from his behaviour that he is a unilateral malformed horse and/or his spinal cord is compromised from his accident.

It took me eight years to write this book – and approximately three boxes of tissues for all the tears and laughter reliving my memories created. I hope it has inspired, entertained, or helped at least one person out there. I was a very insecure teenager who had minimal self-esteem but found my passion to heal and nurture my soul.

We all have a story to tell. Enjoy your journey.

References

Giacomazzo, B 2022 'Inside the horrifying Little Albert experiment that terrified an infant to the point of tears', *all that's interesting*, https://allthatsinteresting.com/little-albert-experiment

Winbrow, D 1934 'The Guy in the Glass Poem (The Man in the Mirror)' in *The American Magazine*

Acknowledgements

All my clients who trusted me with their horses and allowed me to investigate and try to find best outcomes.

Every person I have watched giving a horse clinic.

Every person that has come to one of my clinics.

Every vet, farrier, horse bodyworker, surgeon, acupuncturist, masseuse, chiropractor, vet nurse I have ever met.

I have left out some individuals' real names in case I have not put them in the amazing light I feel they deserve. Those individuals know how much I thank them for always assisting me with my million questions and need for explanations.

Head Honcho and Production Wiz, Kev and Les, from Busybird Publishing. You guys rock and have been a wealth of knowledge, advice and support. Thank you for helping me get my story out.

Last, but, as they say, definitely not least, to my supportive and amazing husband and kids, thank you. You make me happy and proud every day.

About the Author

Carmen Volz is a holistic horse trainer who has had her own business doing this for the last 20 years. She is a first-time author of "My Journey with Horses". With over 40 years' experience in the horse industry, and having dealt with many difficulties in her life, she brings a soulful, realistic and personal approach to her writing by wanting to help other people and horses.

www.ingramcontent.com/pod-product-compliance
Lightning Source LLC
Chambersburg PA
CBHW061215070526
44584CB00029B/3848